THE PRINCETON REVIEW

How to Survive Without Your Parents' Money

THE PRINCETON REVIEW

How to Survive Without Your Parents' Money

Making it from College to the "Real World"

By Geoff Martz

RANDOM HOUSE
NEW YORK   1996
http://www.randomhouse.com

Princeton Review Publishing, L.L.C.
2315 Broadway, 3rd Floor
New York, NY 10024
E-mail: info@review.com

Library of Congress Cataloging-in-Publication Data

Edited by Amy Zavatto and Margaret Balistreri
Designed by the Mac Lab

ISBN 0-679-76984-6

Manufactured in the United States of America on partially
recycled paper.

9 8 7 6 5 4 3 2 1

ACKNOWLEDGMENTS

Thanks to all the great people who were willing to share their entertaining first job experiences (that appear in the margins of this book); to John Katzman, Alicia Ernst, Cynthia Brantley, Margaret Balistreri, Amy Zavatto, Julian Ham, and the crew at The Princeton Review; and to my parents, whose money was always on me, regardless of the point spread.

Contents

Introduction

Naturally, you began this process years ago. You started with a paper route, waking up at dawn every morning, and using your salary to buy food for the poor. This led to a recommendation from the mayor, which landed you a prestigious internship clerking for the Supreme Court while you were still in the third grade.

Mother Teresa and Colin Powell wrote your college recommendations, and by your junior year, you spoke three languages fluently and numbered the CEOs of twenty major corporations among your closest friends.

Or maybe, like most of us, you *meant* to do all this, but somehow didn't get around to it.

No matter how well prepared we are, *no* one ever really feels ready or qualified to hold a job. After all, we know ourselves too well. We know we got a C– in German that time. We know that under our interviewing jacket, the cuff of our best shirt is held together with a safety pin. And when we're sitting looking at the blank piece of paper that we have to turn into a resume, it's easy to feel that *without* the personal friendship of twenty CEOs of major corporations, and many *other* accomplishments we don't have, there is really no point in even trying. Which helps to explain the popularity of graduate school.

The point is that everyone feels this way. If you're feeling slightly nauseous right now, that's normal. You've never done this before.

No doubt you've been told, "*It's tough out there.*" You probably know the litany of woes by heart: new graduates today are competing not just with each other, but with more experienced older workers who've been laid off; new technology is rendering entire professions obsolete; recruitment on campus is down; the unemployment rate among twentysomethings is up.

In fact, each of the dire facts mentioned above has an upside. Sure, new graduates are competing with laid-off experienced workers, but in the eyes of employers, new graduates have an enormous advantage: they're cheaper, and they're too new to have bad habits.

And yes, it's true that an entire profession sometimes does become obsolete through a technological innovation, but this never happens without warning—offering unusual opportunities for those who aren't too busy wringing their hands.

And while getting recruited on campus is an incredibly painless way to get a job, it often means you haven't had a chance to explore all the possibilities and make sure this is the right job (not to mention the right profession) for you.

Fortunately, as any professional stockbroker would be glad to tell you if she thought you had any money, markets are cyclical; when everyone is telling you how awful things are—it generally means they're already getting better.

Besides, during your professional life you're going to be looking for a job more than once. Sometimes the economy will happen to be healthy, sometimes it won't. The point is to learn job-hunting skills that will make the state of the economy irrelevant.

That is what this book is designed to help you do.

You may think making good career decisions is like perfect pitch: you either have it or you don't. But in fact, job hunting skills are completely learnable. It's not a matter of being talented at finding a job; it's a matter of learning to bring your own particular talents (whatever they are) to bear on the job search.

Along the way, you will encounter many strange and foreign concepts out there that you may never have had to deal with before: Con Ed bills, rent, student-loan payments. Many people panic when they move into their first apartment, go looking for the cafeteria, and discover that there is *no meal plan at all*.

But all that pales beside the really scary part. Just when you need them the most, just when you were finally about to forgive them for all the butting in they did when you were growing up, just when you were finally comfortable about letting them help you out with a few dollars here and there, your parents are going to start acting like you are a completed project, a finished sculpture ready to be sent to the kiln for glazing, and they can now buy a Winnebago and travel across the country.

Before you can even blink, they've converted your old bedroom into a sewing nook.

Don't worry. While this book may not take the place of the years of therapy you're going to need to get over being abandoned by your parents, it will at least get you started on your quest for gainful, meaningful employment.

The Class of '95

40% had jobs at graduation

30% had jobs 6 months later

10% were unemployed 6 months later

20% were in graduate school

(Source: Michigan State University Employment Survey, 1995)

First line of Rodney Dangerfield's commencement address in the movie *Back to School*:

"I have only one thing to say to you today as you go out into the world: Don't go."

"Résumés over there."

Drawing by Cheney; ©1992 New York Magazine, Inc.

What "They" Want

In choosing a career, you might think that your most important consideration would be deciding what *you* want; however, if you're like most people, you will spend a good portion of your waking hours worrying instead about what "they" want.

> *"I hear they're looking only for engineers this year."*

> *"They invite you to an interview only if your GPA is above 3.2."*

> *"They'll look at your script only if you have an agent."*

> *"They want only government majors."*

These are all quotes from college seniors interviewed in or outside their college career centers this year. So are these:

"They'll kill me if I don't go to law school."

"He wants me to join the family business."

"They've made a lot of sacrifices for me."

"They" can be parents, prospective employers, society at large, girlfriends, boyfriends—hey, let's face it, when it comes down to putting our future on the line, almost anybody's opinion can seem more important than our own. We visit career counselors, go on informational interviews, consult friends of our parents, consult our parents, surreptitiously check out our horoscopes, ask our own friends, and then, likely as not, when someone actually offers us a job, we take it immediately in a frenzy of gratitude, before the employer has a chance to change his mind.

What we are saying is that a little reflection might be in order here, before you decide to accept a position strip-mining national parks or as a harpooner on a Japanese whaling ship. Let's take a look at what "they" actually want.

WHAT PARENTS WANT

- They want you to be happy. Of course, they would never conceive that you could be happy living in a lifestyle that differs in any way from their own.

- They want nothing less for you than total financial and emotional security *right now*. Next year is not soon enough. Five years from now is out of the question.

- They don't want to have to worry about you anymore. But they will be terribly insulted if you don't call them all the time and share with them your deepest problems.

- They want you to act like an adult. Of course, when you come over for dinner they will treat you like a twelve-year-old child.

- They want you to raise several children *and* have a fulfilling career, but they don't want you to work too hard.

- They want you to maintain the family position. Or they want you to surpass it. Or they don't want you to surpass it.

- They want to be able to brag about you. But not to worry—they will find something to brag about no matter what you do. ("She's personally razed two hundred acres of national forest! Who knew she had such a genius for destruction?")

- They want you not to need them anymore. But they will always be there for you.

As you can see, parents spend a lot of their time feeling conflicted about their grown-up children, and these feelings only get more complicated as you and they get older. However, if they didn't leave you out on a hillside when you hit your "terrible two's," they probably won't disown you now if you take off in a career direction slightly different from the one they had planned for you.

Ultimately, what parents really want is to hear you talking about your work with a sense of accomplishment and purpose. To see you gaining confidence in your own opinion as you get to take on increased responsibility and as you become your own person. It really won't matter what you do. They will love you even if you become a harpooner of whales.

But don't expect them to admit that *now*.

"YOU'RE NOT GETTING ANY YOUNGER, YOU KNOW"

Allan Wolk went straight to law school after he graduated from college. However, after getting his law degree from Boston University, he realized that what he really wanted to do was to get into the creative end of advertising. "I put together a book [which is a portfolio of ads for real and made-up products] with a lot of advice from a teacher. It took about six months. Four months after that I had my first job." How did he go about looking? "In advertising, there's something called *The Red Book*—a lot of industries have something similar—that lists all the different advertising agencies, and the names of the officers of the company. I would find somebody with a friendly sounding name, and I would call them. Of course, with any creative endeavor, everyone has his own opinion about what he likes and doesn't like, which can be pretty devastating when you're new and you don't know who to trust. I made the decision to trust only my teacher.

"When somebody said they liked my work but didn't have any openings right now, I would ask them, 'Do you know of anybody else who's looking?' And that's how I eventually got my first job. Somebody sent me to somebody else, and that man sent me to a *third* person at Jordan, McGrath, who wound up hiring me."

Your family will appear to be obsessed with the straight-line, arrowlike precision of your career path. No side-trips will be acceptable, and once you are committed, never mind how harebrainedly, to a particular job, there can be (in their mind) no turning back. Remember that when they began their careers there was a lot more loyalty between employee and employer. Many people in those days retired after thirty years or so without ever having switched companies. Parents understand that things have changed (in fact, one or both of them has probably been laid off in the last five years, according to the Bureau of Labor Statistics), but that doesn't mean they like the new rules, and old advice dies hard.

It is also important to remember that they grew up in a time of enormous prosperity. The U.S. economy soared after World War II, and didn't falter in any significant way until the 1970s. Many of our parents have led charmed lives: they entered college when admission was less competitive; they entered the job market when the economy was booming; they bought houses just in time to see the real-estate market take off; and then they invested just as interest rates soared. About the only reason to feel sorry for them is that your college education just cost them about fifteen times what their parents paid for theirs.

Again, your parents know that the rules have changed. The economy today is in a different place, and jobs are somewhat harder to come by. They read the papers (and have probably clipped and saved all the gloomiest articles for you to read). But paradoxically, this will just make them that much more determined that your only course is a conservative one. They want you to be taken care of, settled, as soon as possible, and in their haste, they may ignore what's best for you—in other words, what *you* want.

It is no use reminding them that in their youth, they may not have known exactly what they wanted to do either. That they may have had several false starts before they discovered their ideal profession. That they took risks, too. They have forgotten all this, and it is simply unacceptable to them that you should take any risks at all.

The Family Agenda

It may not entirely surprise you to learn that your family already has some quite specific thoughts about what you should and should not do with the rest of your life. You may have detected this in subtle, delicately reasoned, conversational remarks like, "How can you say you want to be a nuclear scientist, when you can't even keep your room clean?" Or you may have suspected your father was trying to tell you something when he said, "You'll go into politics over my dead body." Your parents' ideas for your future are not confined simply to what they don't want you to do. They also know what they want you to do and will point to your childhood accomplishments as evidence: "I knew when you were a little girl and you cut off your Barbie's arm with a hatchet that you would one day be a surgeon."

The confusing part is that sometimes they turn out to be right. After all, they *have* known you for a long time. They know what subjects you did best in at school, and what topics most animated you at the dinner table. They know whether you are a self-starter or whether you do best when you are given assignments. In other words, they know a lot of things you may be pushing to the back of your mind because they don't fit *your* mental picture of the career you want to pursue.

On the other hand, they may be trying to fit you into *their* mental picture based on childhood interests that you have long since outgrown.

To make things even more confusing, you may have a career that seems to run in your family; or perhaps there is a family firm that you are expected to join; or maybe your family doesn't care exactly what kind of job you take, so long as it is within certain, shall we say, tolerances. "It doesn't matter what you do, just so long as you earn $100,000 a year." Now again it may turn out that your family's agenda is, in fact, your agenda as well. After all, you grew up with this family. It wouldn't be surprising if you shared some of the same values. Growing up in a particular environment will certainly affect your ideas of what is possible in life.

For example, if you were raised in the environment of academia, it is certainly easier to imagine yourself in that field than in an environment you have never

---

Number of women at the top

1980—out of 6,400 executive officers and directors in the United States, there were ten women.

1990—out of 4,000 executive officers and directors in the United States, nineteen were women.

(Fortune, 1990)

experienced. In many ways, the child of a professor would have a real advantage in an academic setting. You already know the lifestyle. Even without realizing it, you have probably picked up the rules and the etiquette of university life. But whatever your family's agenda, you owe it to yourself to at least question whether the traditional family occupation is the correct course for you.

Ultimately, what they want is for you to be happy, and as soon as they see that you know what you want to do and are happy doing it, they will be happy as well.

What Employers Want

"It's like being pregnant—you can read about it and think about it a lot, but nothing is going to prepare you for the experience of your first job except doing it. People think showbiz is a glamorous, exciting world, but in fact it's like that maybe twice a year. The rest of the time is full of hard, lugubrious work."

(Anonymous television producer)

Believe it or not, if you are a recent college graduate, you already have the number one attribute employers are seeking in an entry-level hire. You are brand new. To put it bluntly, they want your youth. When a company decides to hire a new graduate, it is buying his newness, his just-out-of-the-box optimism, his willingness to work hard for not much money. When a company decides to hire a new graduate, it is buying her willingness to learn, her ability to be flexible, her desire to excel. An entry-level employee is not really expected to know anything yet. Thus you are being hired not so much for your skills as for your promise.

Well, every twentysomething has promise.

So what else do they want? We asked a number of employers to share their wish list with us. The results were surprising. It didn't seem to matter whether they were from an investment bank, a law firm, an advertising agency, a TV soap opera, a design firm, or an entertainment magazine; they all turned out to be looking for the same thing. Now, you might be saying, "That's ridiculous. Those jobs all require different qualifications." Sure, these employers all may have been looking for different kinds of summer work experience, and some were looking at GPAs while others were more interested in coursework—but they were all basically hoping that the same kind of young woman or man was going to come walking through their door. Here's what they said they wanted:

PASSION

Everybody said it differently, but they were all saying the same thing. The investment banker called it curiosity: "I want to know if people are curious. I often think about what it takes to be successful where we are. The ones who're curious enough to ask, 'Couldn't we do this another way?'—these are the people who will have the hunger and tenacity to make it in our field."

The soap opera producer called it passion. "I don't expect them to know what they want *exactly* yet, but I need to feel that they are passionate about something. I ask them, 'If I were your fairy godmother and could tap you on the shoulder and turn you into anything you wanted, what would it be?' I don't care exactly what their dream is, but I want them to have one, whether it's directing or writing or producing."

The lawyer called it "that intangible fire in the belly." At his firm, new college graduates are regularly hired as paralegals. "Mostly, I look for someone who wants to learn and is willing to learn." How can employers tell if someone has the "fire"? "It's a gut thing."

Of course there are *some* tangible clues to look for. A curious person probably has taken the time to find out quite a lot about the company she is interviewing with, and the industry as a whole—*before* she walks into an interview. A curious person has probably also cultivated a wide range of outside interests. Let's face it; you can generally spot a curious, passionate, fire-in-the-belly sort of person at twenty paces.

Highest Salaries Paid to Dead People	
Elvis Presley	$15 million
Ian Fleming	$7.5
John Lennon	$5.0
Jimi Hendrix	$4.0
T.S. Eliot	$2.5
James Dean	$1.2
Jim Morrison	$1.0
Marilyn Monroe	$1.0
John Wayne	$.7
Abbott and Costello	$.4

(Forbes, 1990)

THE PERFECT CANDIDATE

There are people who just walk down the street, and when you see them you feel good about them. *You* know what we mean. If you were selling ice cream, you would want to give them free ice cream. If you had a decision to make, you would want to ask their opinion. If you were a personnel director, you would want to give them jobs.

If you are one of these people, then you don't need this book. Put it back on the shelf, and turn around. There is probably a *Fortune 500*–company CEO right behind you who is just about to say:

"Excuse me, but I couldn't help noticing that you are looking for a job."

"I'm not looking for someone who comes in and tells me how stupid everybody else is or how screwed up they are. Unless the gossip is really good, of course, in which case I make an exception."

(Anonymous magazine editor)

However, if you are like the rest of us, you have moments when you feel invincible, and moments when you would not dream of even getting out of bed.

Of course, all employers are different, and not all of them are going to like the same people. However, if you are coming off as a person who is confident, happy about who you are, interested in life, and conscientious, then you are going to connect more times than not.

We don't all carry our virtues on our sleeve like that. In fact, some people who stride down the street like they are on their way to sign a multimillion-dollar contract or cure cancer are odious, insecure people we wouldn't wish on our worst enemies.

You might be able to learn to *act* like a junior power broker even if you feel worthless, but there is a better way. We don't want to sound like some Windham Hill version of "Kumbaya" here, but the thing most employers want is to sense that *you* know what *you* want.

We *all* exude passion when we're fascinated about something and can't wait to learn more. So the trick is to find the one thing that you find terribly interesting and important, and look for a job in that area. In the next chapter we'll show you how to do that, but before we do, the employers we interviewed had some other things on their wish list.

EXPERIENCE

"Great, so you have a college degree. Big fucking deal. New graduates have to realize they don't know anything yet, and learn to become part of the team."

(Anonymous employer)

Having found a way to get some previous experience, even before you finished college, indicates your passion for a career. "It tells me they're interested," says an editor at an entertainment magazine. "Real experience helps, whether it's on a college paper's copy desk or as an intern at a newspaper. I'd like to see some clips from a community newspaper, or a college newspaper—even a term paper if it is particularly well written."

FLEXIBILITY

Times being what they are, if you are sincerely interested in a particularly sought-after field, you may have to start at the very bottom. According to an account manager at a large advertising firm, "even though the economy is doing better, people are still having to come in the back door, because the training programs have been cut. Take my secretary, now. He's wonderful, a college grad, and has all the determination and energy to get on. He's working as my secretary because it was the only way to get in the door." Are these jobs actually promotable? "If you really have it, I think it's recognized right away."

The soap opera producer agrees that people have to be patient. "If I hire someone as a production coordinator, which is how I started, he may be stuck in that position for two years these days. It was much easier ten years ago. I moved up after eight months."

GREAT ATTITUDE

Entry-level jobs are not always glamorous, and employers don't want to feel they have to apologize for asking you to do some photocopying. "New hires don't realize that we *all* have to do paperwork. That's what life is all about," says the investment banker. "We all do nonsense work. People expect that there are secretaries that handle all the scud work."

A great attitude means being willing to do the "scud" work without complaining. As the lawyer puts it: "If I had to give one piece of advice to people just starting out—perky is better."

PEOPLE SKILLS

Even if you're a talented genius in your field, you won't get far in the work world without the ability to get along with and motivate your co-workers. "Because I've been in the industry for a long time, I know what type of personality is going to mesh with our situation," says the manager of a large New York design firm. "I don't necessarily look at grades or schools. Obviously, a design background or experience in the industry is helpful, but a new graduate isn't going to have much experience,

Number of 22-year-olds in 1990:

3,641,000

Number of 22-year-olds in 1990 with bachelor's degrees:

1,043,000

Projected number of 22-year-olds in the year 2000:

3,549,000

Projected number of 22-year-olds in the year 2000 with bachelor's degrees:

1,129,000

(Source: Monthly Labor Review, July 1992)

and I'm only going to start them out in showroom positions anyway. So what's important to me are people skills, how they present themselves."

THE ABILITY TO HANDLE ADVERSITY

Grace under pressure is a particularly prized commodity in fast-paced, deadline-driven professions. "We often look for team sports," says the investment banker, "because how you deal with failures has a lot to do with how you deal with losing. Do you sulk? How do you move the team forward? If you played a sport in college, I will frequently ask about your team's record. If the team had a lot of losses, I'll ask what it's like to practice and drill when your team never wins."

A PERFECTIONIST . . .

"The work world is perfectionist oriented," says the investment banker. They all agreed. "I need people who are compulsive, because we're constantly dealing with crises," said the producer. "They have to pay a lot of attention to detail," said the designer.

. . . IN AN EASYGOING, NONCOMPULSIVE WAY

"But they can't be robots," said the same designer. "They have to be human."

STEADY PERFORMANCE

"That's a big one," according to the lawyer. In college it is often easy to disguise an uneven performance. If you miss a couple of weeks of class in a particular course, you can still ace the final. If you didn't start work on your paper until the night before it's due, you can pull an all-nighter. And with a few exceptions, you probably worked alone, without the need to get along or interact on a professional level with people with whom you had little in common.

In the real world, there is no place to hide. You have to turn up every day, smelling reasonably good, in freshly ironed clothes. You have to make conversation with your

"I recently had to hire someone. It came down to two people. This one kid had better skills, but he was whiny. Now, I don't need that. Ultimately, I'm going to be spending a lot of time with this person. There is a lot of interaction in an office. So I hired the other one, and she's working out great."

(Anonymous employer)

boss every day, and at any time you may be called upon to perform strenuous mental tasks that you didn't even know were coming up when you arrived in the morning. In other words, there is a minimum level of daily competency below which you cannot fall. The level is different in every office, but no amount of spotty brilliance will make up for one really costly error you made on one of your bad days. In the professional world, reliability is not just prized, it is often required.

There are lots of differences between college and the workplace, but probably the most important one is that in college, *you* were the customer. If you screwed up, your professors would probably forgive you because, after all, you were paying. College is not unlike those health spas in the desert, where you spend huge amounts of money for the privilege of working like a dog and being served really awful food, but in the end you feel much better. If there was one night when you couldn't take it anymore, and slipped out for a hot-fudge sundae, they had to forgive you because you were the customer.

In the work world, someone *else* is the customer. You are being paid to solve their problems, and if they are nasty, or make exorbitant demands on you, they think you have to forgive them because, after all, they are paying *you*.

WHAT ABOUT GRADES?

"Grades signify a desire to achieve," said the investment banker. "We want people for whom doing the best is important, and that's going to be reflected by their GPA." In general, financial and engineering companies look quite closely at academic records. Other employers are less impressed. "I don't care about grades or where they went to school," says the producer. Of course, no employer will completely ignore good grades.

WHAT THEY WANT

These are the traits all the employers seemed to agree on (except for grades)—the universal characteristics that would get you a job in any field. Like parents, employers sometimes are a little conflicted about what they want from you as well:

- They want your youth, but they expect you to be very mature.

- They want you to be loyal to them. On the other hand, they expect you to go away when they don't need you anymore.

- They want you to be aggressive and a self-starter, but not too aggressive or too much of a self-starter.

- They want you to be inquisitive but not overbearing.

- They want you to make them look good for having hired you, but they don't want you to make them look too good about having hired you.

In the end, it all boils down to this: they want you to be tremendously interested in the field you want to enter; to illustrate that you care enough to inform yourself about it; to be willing to work hard and acquire the skills necessary to get the job in the first place; to be well rounded and easy to work with. They want your passion.

But mostly what they want is for you to act like you know what *you* want.

What You Want

Figuring out what you actually want to do, exactly, for the rest of your life can seem like a pretty daunting task. Many people get temporarily paralyzed worrying about making the right decision.

Well, we can completely set your mind at ease about this. Even if you actually could find the perfect job, statistics say you won't be able to keep it, anyway. According to the authors of *Workplace 2000: The Revolution Reshaping American Business*, Americans who begin their careers in the 1990s will probably hold ten or more different jobs for five or more employers—and, according to the U.S. Department of Labor, they may have to shift careers (not just jobs—*careers*) as many as four times.

So take some heat off yourself. No *one* job is going to be your final destination, and that's a good thing. Jumping from one company or organization to another will sometimes get you salary increases, new challenges, and more responsibility. But there's jumping and then there's *jumping*.

For people who don't have a clear idea of what they want, there may not be much continuity running through their working lives. A person might start off as a salesperson, then take a position as a middle manager, and end up in advertising, and each new job may simply have been a reaction to having lost the one before.

On the other hand, people who actually know what they want will be able to develop a through-line in their work life, so that their career becomes a series of logical steps taken thoughtfully as they explore the different facets of their talents and of their chosen field. The U.S. Department of Labor statistics we mentioned—like all statistics—are describing what will happen to *most* people. You are not most people. How do we know? For one thing, you're taking the trouble to read this book.

BE CAREFUL WHAT YOU ASK FOR . . .

By spending a little time now reflecting on what it is you want, you will stand a better chance of getting it. Not everyone is going to be shifting careers four times. People who feel fulfilled by what they do, and are extremely good at what they do, are not the ones who generally get let go in hard times. They have already made themselves indispensable. It's the people who show up because they have to but who aren't really happy about what they do—these are the ones who end up looking through the help-wanted ads again and again.

Of course, it is not just downshifts in the economy that can cause upheavals. These days, technological innovations can render whole industries obsolete in just a few years, or create entire new industries where none existed before. However, if you are totally involved in and fascinated by your profession, you will be one of the first to notice if your company—or your industry—is becoming outmoded, and thus one of the first to see ways to expand or diversify. For example, if you had been in the very lucrative business of supplying law libraries and law firms with the constantly updated reference books they required, you could have wrung your hands in the 1980s as you watched the burgeoning of computer information systems, or you could have done what Mead Data Central did, and started Lexis, a computer on-line program for lawyers, which may well totally replace law libraries in the next few years.

Number of college graduates in the labor force in 1990:

28,983,000

Number of college graduates in the labor force performing jobs that did not require a college degree in 1990:

5,753,000

(Source: Monthly Labor Review, July 1992)

. . . You Might Just Get It

Your career may not have a strict linear progression in the traditional sense—the old images of climbing up one corporate ladder until you reach the top, or fall off, are a little outmoded. What's important is that the progression of your different jobs and responsibilities makes sense to *you*.

Thus, before you embark on a job search, it is a good idea to decide *generally* what you would like to accomplish long-term, and *specifically* what you can do to move toward that goal now. Keep in mind, your ideas of what you want may change gradually as you gain experience. You may become more fascinated by one particular specialized area within your chosen field. For example, an advertising account manager might realize over time that she is more interested in cutting-edge advertising. To attain her slightly altered goal, she might try to get herself assigned to the accounts of younger companies more willing to experiment with boundaries, or she could jump ship to a more innovative advertising firm.

Your goals might also change in reaction to an opportunity you could not possibly have imagined. For example, a car executive might be offered a job working for a federal emissions-control commission. After careful consideration, he might decide he could not resist the challenge of this new opportunity, and be willing to change his goals slightly to take advantage of it.

You might even decide after exploring a particular field for a while that you can better express your talents in another field entirely. For example, a journalist might decide that she would rather help make the news than report it, and therefore decide to take a job working as a speechwriter for a politician.

The First Step

In any case, unless you are either extremely lucky or not very ambitious at all, your first job out of college is not going to be your ultimate goal; it will be the first step toward exploring the field in which you think you might want to spend your life working. It will provide you with the chance to learn about your field, gain professional experience, and zero in on exactly which parts of this profession interest you the most.

Your objective, when you *do* accept a job offer, is to begin building translatable skills you can take with you as you move along your path, including one of the more important skills you can learn: the ability to market yourself successfully when it is time to look for the next job.

Therefore, no matter how vague your career objectives are, your first job will begin the process of exploration that will ultimately lead you to where you want to go. Keep in mind that the more you can narrow down your interests before you start your job search, the faster you will be able to get there, and the less chance that you will get lost along the way.

It is easy to panic and take the first job that comes along. However, no one should ever take what Douglas Coupland calls a "McJob" for any other reason than temporary sustenance. A "McJob" (he defines it as a "low-pay, low-prestige, low-benefit, no-future job in the service sector, frequently considered a satisfying career choice by people who have never held one") will never get you anywhere, but can seem so soothing and non-threatening, that some McJob holders wake up five years later and find themselves in the same spot, only older.

Frankly, it is better to begin the process of defining your career objectives now, before you get locked into inflexible thinking. The earlier you start, the sooner you will find yourself where you want to be. Besides, defining your career objectives gets easier with practice. So let's get specific. What do you want?

What the 5,753,000 college graduates who are performing jobs that do not require a college degree are actually doing:	
Retail sales	644,000
Sales supervisor	502,000
Administrative	1,533,000
Blue collar	1,306,000
Service industry	889,000
Farm	190,000
Unemployed	688,000

(Source: Monthly Labor Review, July 1992)

IF YOU'RE LIKE MOST OF US, YOU WANT . . .

- Wealth beyond measure.

- The respect—no, let's be honest—the *awe* of your co-workers and bosses.

- Total mastery of your profession, so long as it doesn't cut into your social life.

- Absolute power over all that you survey, although you don't ever want to have to actually fire anybody.

- Lots of little people to do all the boring routine work, leaving you free to concentrate on the important, glamorous decisions.

Money, status, and power—did we leave anything out? Okay, so this list may have to be revised *a little*. Many people see the above items as goals in and of themselves. In fact, all these things—including status, power, and wealth—are actually just by-products of something much more important: an occupation that fulfills you and makes you happy.

There are people out there who are able to pursue wealth for wealth's sake or fame for fame's sake. But for the most part, when you read articles about successful people, what most interests them about their professions are the intellectual challenges inherent in what they do. You may think it's lip service when a famous movie star says in an interview:

> *"I'm just happy to be allowed to act. I'd do it for free."*

Fortunately, actors have agents to call up the studios the next day and explain, "He was just kidding. We want $3 million plus a percentage of the gross."

But in fact, he probably wasn't kidding. Successful people are generally so interested in what they do that they *would* do it for free if they had to.

Don't worry, you won't have to.

TOO MANY CHOICES

There are lots of books out there designed to help you figure out what you want to do with your life. Perhaps the best of them is *What Color Is Your Parachute?* by Richard Bolles, which, like its lesser competitors, gives you many exercises to help you discover your inner feelings and hidden talents. We think one of the greatest features of these books is that doing all the exercises

---

The five richest young people in America

1. William Henry Gates (Microsoft), 39 years old, $15 billion

2. Steven Anthony Ballmer (Microsoft), 39 years old, $2.9 billion

3. Theodore W. Waitt (Gateway 2000) 32 years old, $1 billion

4. Stuart Robert Levine (Cabletron Systems), 37 years old, $780 million

5. Michael Dell (Dell Computer), 30 years old, $740 million

6, 7, and 8. Dirk, Robert, and Daniel Ziff (Ziff Communications heirs), 31, 29, and 23 years old, together share $2 billion

9. Raymond Harbert (inheritance), 36 years old $600 million

10. Carline Marie Getty (inheritance), 38 years old, $570 million

properly could take you several thoughtful, interesting, self-revealing, spiritual months. In other words, these books can be wonderful ways to *procrastinate*. After all, you can't be expected to go looking for a job if you don't know what you're looking for. So, during the time you are searching your soul, you can happily putter around at home, and it's okay because it's all part of a master plan.

If you really have no idea what you are interested in, you should buy the Bolles book, and take advantage of the career counseling at your college's career center (see chapter 4) or hire a career counselor (see chapter 8).

But you probably do have an idea. Maybe it's part of a long-nourished childhood dream; perhaps it came out of a summer work experience or a particular course in college; perhaps there is a person you have always admired and would like to emulate. Your idea may already be crystal clear in your head, or it may not be completely formed.

You are looking for the thing that interests you so much that you are willing to spend eight hours a day (at the very least) in its pursuit.

TALENTS VS. TEMPERAMENT

Knowing what you want comes from an understanding of the interplay of two important things: your talents and your temperament. By talents, we are not talking about something as specific as your ability to trade bonds. You've never had a chance to trade bonds, so how would you know if you're any good at it? We mean general talents, such as "being good with numbers" or "performing well under pressure."

Once you've acknowledged what your talents are, you can think about how those talents would help you in the fields to which your temperament is leading you. By temperament, we mean your personal inclinations in terms of lifestyle, environment, and social status. Some examples of temperament: "I want to drive a Porsche" or "I'm flexible about a job, just so long as it's near a great beach" or "I want to work for a socially conscious organization."

Let's take the person who is "good with numbers" and "performs well under pressure." These talents could be used in many different ways. If her temperament inclined her toward economic comfort, she might in fact become a bond trader. However, if her temperament inclined her toward social consciousness, she might be more tempted to use the same talents to become a nonprofit fund-raiser, or a stock fraud investigator.

ASSESSING YOUR TALENTS

Let's break this up into two parts.

PART ONE: WHAT YOU'VE BEEN TOLD YOU'RE GOOD AT

It's important to pay attention to what other people think your talents are, because outside observers can sometimes spot things you're too close to see. If you had decided to become a concert violinist when you were seven, you may never have noticed that the boogie-woogie piano you play for relaxation packs a lot more oomph than your Mozart. Feedback from teachers or friends can be invaluable in pointing out where your greatest strengths lie—just so long as you remember that this feedback may come with an agenda attached. Some teachers and parents like to proselytize: they may want to convert you to their career choice, convince you to follow in their footsteps. Some friends may want you to follow or lead them in a particular direction as well, and *everyone's* opinion comes complete with their own value judgments.

You might want to find a piece of paper and jot down what other people have told you you were good at over the years. Start with when you were a small child and work forward. These talents will not necessarily be job-related—at least not on the surface. For example, if you got praise for making the peace between two of your friends in second grade, that might be an early indicator of a talent for mediation. Write down everything you can think of. None of these memories is going to surprise you—we're not expecting you to have some kind of primal epiphany where you suddenly dredge up a long-repressed urge to be a microbiologist—but your memories of what other people saw as your talents when you were growing up might help you to clarify your goals.

PART TWO: WHAT YOU THINK YOU'RE GOOD AT OR MIGHT BE GOOD AT

Even if you've always wanted to become an airline pilot, you may never have had the opportunity to fly a plane. This does not mean you have no talent for flying. It simply means your talent in this direction has not yet had a chance to show itself. Write down on that piece of paper the talents you *suspect* you might have.

Let's not forget that a lot of the time, what passes for talent is really just passion, anyway. A person with a passion for any field is going to spend the time needed to get good at it.

You may have developed your interest in a particular field as a result of daydreaming, a book you've read, a summer job, or even a television show. No matter how silly the initial source of your interest, you should not automatically dismiss it. It's up to you to discover if this interest could become a passion.

Here's a small sampling of the different kinds of talents you might have written down to describe yourself.

I am good at, or *think* I could be good at, or people *say* I am good at:

organization, attention to detail, innovative thinking, intuitive thinking, performing well under pressure, manipulating numbers, scientific analysis, writing, drawing or painting, public speaking, working with other people, working alone, convincing other people, teaching other people.

ASSESSING YOUR TEMPERAMENT

What kind of lifestyle do you want? Where do you want to live? What kind of culture do you want to be part of? Choosing a career is a matter of examining your innate talents in light of your temperament.

WHAT KIND OF LIFESTYLE DO YOU WANT?

Each profession often has its own particular lifestyle—a fact that many new graduates seldom give much thought to before they arrive for their first day. Do you mind being frantically busy, with frequent late nights, or would you rather live a more sedate life? Are you single and willing to travel or are you more interested in settling down and raising a family right away? These are legitimate questions to ask yourself before you start the interviewing process. Even within particular professions, you will find that different companies can provide completely different lifestyles. Someone interested in journalism, for example, could choose to work for a daily newspaper with constant deadlines (and perhaps a correspondingly high level of excitement) or he could choose to work for a monthly, with more leisurely deadlines (and perhaps a higher quotient for in-depth, reflective writing).

Is it important to you to be financially well-off? While most professions offer at least the chance of becoming rich, some are more likely bets than others. Few poets have ever gotten wealthy off their sonnets. Now, wealth for wealth's sake is empty and hollow (or so we've heard), but some professionals live much more comfortably than others.

Are you willing to take risks or are you risk-averse? Some professions (futures trading, lion taming) involve constant small risks. Others (acting, songwriting, painting) involve what is in some ways a larger risk: the possibility that you will never be discovered or acknowledged for what you do, at least not in your own lifetime.

Irving Botwinick wanted nothing more that to work in the garment industry. "I thought that would be the most exciting thing in the world, but they only wanted experience, and I didn't have any." Irving called on many firms in the garment district, but came up empty. "Finally, I walk into this one office and I tell the woman at the desk, 'I want to see the boss. I've got something you can't refuse.' The boss came out, and I said, 'I want to work here so much that I'll work for you for free for two weeks, and if you don't like me, you can just tell me to get lost, but if you like me, then you have to give me a job.'

"He hired me on the spot. Two weeks later he hired me permanently, and two weeks after *that*, he gave me a raise."

WHERE DO YOU WANT TO LIVE?

You may not have total say over where you live, at least not in the beginning, but you should certainly think about what kind of physical environment would make you happiest. This is not just a matter of city vs. country. What *kind* of city? Los Angeles is supposed to be "laid-back." New York is jangly. Miami is hot. Minneapolis is a great place to raise a family. If you're thinking that you would be happiest in a country setting, what does that mean to you? A farm in Maine, or just a reasonably rural suburban development with some trees? Are you willing to work overseas?

WHAT KIND OF CULTURE DO YOU WANT TO BE PART OF?

Every profession has its own culture. Software designers living in the relaxed atmosphere of Silicon Valley come to work in T-shirts and jeans (and seldom go home). In the hip world of advertising, style is at a premium, but there often exists an urbane informality in the workplace. At certain banks in New York, the dress code is so rigid that you can see five men get out of an elevator wearing identical suits.

None of this may seem important to you right now, but to some degree your acceptance of a particular job is also an implicit acceptance of its culture.

Part of your exploration of a career should include not just a look at the business itself but also a close look at the *way* that business is conducted. Different companies have different standards of ethics and morality; you will be a lot happier if you explore this with yourself before you accept a job. Some businesses are run exclusively by the bottom line, and may expect you to operate the same way. Others bend over backward to preserve tradition and fairhandedness—or, at least, political correctness.

Executive Perks		
Benefit	Percent of companies	
	1987	1991
Company Plane	21%	17%
Car Phone	14%	30%
Reserved Parking	54%	44%
Dining Club	41%	28%
Country Club	42%	35%

(Source: *Business Week*, September 1992)

HOW DO YOU FIND OUT IF A PARTICULAR PROFESSION OR COMPANY WILL SUIT YOUR TEMPERAMENT?

Immerse yourself in their world. Start by looking through your local newspaper and national magazines for stories that relate to your prospective profession. You will be surprised to discover how many news stories have a direct impact on your field. The business section in particular can be very useful.

However, even more useful than general-interest publications are the trade newspapers, magazines, and newsletters that specialize in your field. Every profession has its bible. For business types, *The Wall Street Journal* is a must-read. For entertainment types, it is *Variety* and *Billboard*. To find out the bible for your particular field, you can either ask someone in the field to recommend the trade publications she reads, or go to the library and look in a book called the *Gale Directory of Publications and Broadcast Media*. Some professional organizations (such as the Director's Guild) while quite difficult to get into, will allow newcomers to subscribe to their professional journal, which is a great way to find out what is going on in the field. Read these publications cover to cover—not just the news articles, but the features and the classified ads in the back as well.

Many of these publications now have internet web pages, and many of the companies themselves are following suit. (For more on this, see chapter 7.)

Even a popular novel or memoir that is set in the professional world you are interested in can be extremely valuable. For example, *Liar's Poker*, the true-life experiences of a young man in investment banking, will give you one man's entertaining take on what that world is like.

THE INFORMATIONAL INTERVIEW

Another way to get a firsthand look at a profession is to go on an informational interview. We'll cover this in more detail in our chapter on interviewing, but it deserves a brief mention here because it can also help you to understand the *culture* of a profession.

Unlike the standard interview—essentially an audition for a job—an informational interview is generally set up by a person who has not yet started looking for a job. Let's say you're curious about the insurance industry and you want to know more about what it would be like to work in the field. You canvass all your friends and family for possible connections to people who work in insurance; you write letters to recent alumni from your school who went into the industry; maybe you've read an interesting article about a maverick figure in insurance, so you write her a fan letter. And you politely ask each of these people whether it would be possible for you to come and talk to them. You make it plain you are not yet in the market for a job. You merely want to know more about insurance.

You might think employed people would have better things to do than give informational interviews, but every boss we talked to said he would be glad to talk to someone on this basis, so long as he was approached correctly.

Where did the 1,000 top CEOs go to college?	
Yale	32
Princeton	31
Harvard	22
U. of Mich.	18
U. Penn.	17
Northwestern	17
Stanford	16
Cornell	16

(Source: Business Week, October 12, 1992)

Which leaves 831 unaccounted for.

In addition to making a great impression so that later you can approach this person again, and in addition to finding out some of the black-and-white details about the insurance industry (or whatever field you are interested in), you also get to discover a bit about the culture of the profession. What was the atmosphere at the office? Did the other employees seem happy? Ask the person you're interviewing what a typical day at his job is like. If he is only a few years out of school himself, so much the better. He'll still remember what it was like to be starting out in an entry-level job.

THE INTERSECTION OF TALENT AND TEMPERAMENT

Knowing what you want to do is what makes you attractive to employers (and people in general) and also what will make you happy. At the intersection of your talent and your temperament you will find that you are so interested by life that you are willing to overcome your shyness, willing to learn and ingest any new information, willing to take risks—and willing to start early.

Starting Early

No matter how early you've started your job search, you're probably already convinced that you're late. If you're reading this page today, you're certain you should have been reading it yesterday. If you're a senior in college, you probably think you should have read it when you were a junior, and if you graduated last year, you're certain you should have read it the year before.

When people think they're already behind, they tend to rush into things—like taking the first job anyone offers them, even if it has nothing to do with the field that really interests them. Of course, this is not necessarily fatal. Lots of people who wander into a particular line of work more or less by accident find that two or three years later they could not conceive of working anywhere else. If you have no strong feeling about what field to go into, even after doing the reflective thinking we talked about in chapter 2, then there is nothing wrong with letting events carry you along. However, if you *do* have a strong leaning toward a particular occupation, then you owe it to yourself to explore that occupation.

Here's the deal. To get an interesting job in a field you love, you have to be able to offer your employers something they want. Now, believe us, you already have many of the things they want: you have youth, optimism, vigor, you're willing to work hard, you aren't burned out yet, and you don't expect a lot of money.

But employers want to have their cake and eat it, too. Even though they value your freshly baked, just-out-of-the-box newness, they somehow expect you to have lots of experience as well. And there's only one way to get that experience: start early.

See what we mean? You're already late.

STARTING EARLY, *WHENEVER* YOU START

No, you're not really late. Starting early is a state of mind. It doesn't matter if you're reading this as a college freshman or whether you are already two years out of school—the point is to start early *now*.

This simply means laying the groundwork for the job you're really looking for. If the people who could give you the job you want won't give it to you until you have some experience, then you'll just have to find a way to get that experience.

Fortunately, there are two fail-safe ways to get experience, even in the most sought-after fields.

INTERNSHIPS AND VOLUNTEER WORK

Each year, thousands of companies in the United States and around the world allow college students and older persons to work as interns or volunteers. In some cases, these internships or volunteer jobs earn you college credit. In rarer cases, internships earn you money. But much more important, these "minijobs" earn you access to fields that would be almost impossible to crack if you were looking for a full-time job.

Whether you're interested in working behind the scenes on a television news program, in the bullpen at an investment bank, as a congressional intern in Washington, D.C., or on an archaeological dig in Nigeria, internships and volunteer jobs represent the back door into the most competitive fields in the job market by providing you with the experience you need. Just as important as the credit on your resume is the opportunity to find out whether you would actually enjoy the day-to-day life in the field you are contemplating.

---

25 best places for African Americans to work

Ameritech (Chicago)
Avon (NY)
AT&T (NY)
Chrysler (Highland Park, MI)
Coca-Cola (Atlanta)
Corning (Corning, NY)
DuPont (Wilmington, DE)
Equitable (NY)
Federal Express (Memphis)
Ford (Dearborn, MI)
Gannett Co. (Arlington, VA)
General Mills (Minneapolis)
General Motors (Detroit)
IBM (Armonk, NY)
Johnson and Johnson (New Brunswick, NJ)
Kellogg (Battle Creek, MI)
Marriott (Wash., D.C.)
McDonalds (Oak Brook, IL)
Merck (Rahway, NJ)
NYNEX (NY)
Pepsi-Cola (Somers, NY)
Phillip Morris (NY)
TIAA-CREFF (NY)
United Airlines (Chicago)
Xerox (Rochester, NY)

(*Black Enterprise*, 1992)

If you've ever wondered, "What would it be like to work for a Japanese bank?" You can go and find out. Michael Goodman did, and discovered during an internship after he graduated from Williams that much as he liked sushi, he did not want to eat it out of a cardboard container as he sat working at his desk until ten o'clock every night. He went into publishing instead.

If you've ever been torn about a career decision ("I know I'm good at numbers, but would working as an actuary bore me to death?"), you can go spend a few months and find out. Lisa Buchman did after she earned her degree at Columbia, and consequently decided to go back to school for her PhD so she could teach at the college level.

YOUR DREAM CAREER MAY NOT BE QUITE WHAT YOU EXPECTED

No matter how much you've read about a particular field, and no matter how glamorous (or unglamorous) it may sound on paper, there is no way to know what it's truly like to work in that field without actually working in that field.

You will learn all kinds of surprising things. For example, contrary to popular wisdom, starving American artists often live in Cleveland or Houston rather than Paris; they can't afford the airfare. On the other hand, certain types of auditors (not *generally* known for their jet-setting lifestyles) get to roam the globe, going over the books of companies located in Monte Carlo, Rio, and New Delhi.

Perhaps the most disappointing realization that every newly hired college graduate has to accept is that even very high-powered executives spend some portion of each day engaged in depressingly humdrum matters. You'd think that there would be peons to take care of the routine paperwork, the billing, the ordering.

Well, come to think of it, there are: newly hired college graduates spend a significant portion of their day dealing with their boss's detritus as well as their own.

Effectiveness of various job-search methods, based on U.S. Department of Labor Survey of unemployed American workers (including non-college graduates)

Method	% employed by second month
Private Employment Agency	25.9
Other Search Methods	24.2
Employer Directly	22.5
Friends/Relatives	22.4
Placed/Answered Ads	19.1
Public Employment Agency	18.7

(Source: *Monthly Labor Review*, December 1992)

Or It May Be Exactly What You Expected

On the other hand, the very first day of your volunteer job or internship may simply confirm all your hunches—that this is exactly what you want to be doing for the rest of your life.

If You Are Still in School

Many students think of internships as only taking place during the summer, but in fact you can set up an internship at any time throughout the year. They can last for as little as a few weeks over January break or up to an entire year.

If You Are Already out of School

Students who are just graduating, or who have already graduated often think they don't have time for an internship, particularly if it doesn't pay. They would rather find a job, any job, even if it has nothing to do with what they suspect they might want to do with the rest of their lives. There may be compelling reasons why you cannot take on an internship, but the least compelling of these (as far as we're concerned) is money.

We can already see you bristling. "What about my student loans? What about my rent?" Listen, most entry-level jobs don't pay very much anyway. A chance to work in your dream occupation may be worth working at night as a waitress or a legal proofreader, at least for a few months. If you aren't sure how to go about finding a seedy night job, you will find lots of advice in chapter 11, "Surviving While You're Looking."

Where to Find an Internship or Volunteer Job

The first place to look for an internship if you're still in school is at your college's career center—a place so important to your future well-being that we have devoted an entire chapter to it right after this one. Your career center receives listings of internships from companies who are particularly interested in applicants from your school.

Fred Bernstein decided not to wait until after he graduated from Princeton to begin pursuing his career in journalism. All through college he wrote campus-related freelance articles for a local newspaper. When he graduated, the newspaper immediately offered him a full-time job.

"Let's put it this way," Fred advises. "If you want to be a journalist and Henry Kissinger comes to speak at your college, write a story and send it out immediately to your local newspaper."

These companies can range from a commuter railroad in Pittsburgh, to an artist management company specializing in classical chamber music ensembles in New York, to an investment bank in Austria, to a nonprofit environmental group in Chicago, to a television production company in Hollywood. (These examples, culled more or less at random, are all actual listings received by various colleges this year.)

If you have already graduated from college, look for the eligibility requirements. You will be amazed at how many of them say "Open to college seniors and career-changers" or "Open to college juniors, seniors, and graduate students including career-changers and people reentering the work force."

However, there are thousands of employers with internships to hand out who specifically say they welcome college graduates. How do you find these companies? There are a number of books out there, but the best two (if we do say so ourselves) are *The Princeton Review Student Access Guide to America's Top Internships*, and *The Princeton Review Internship Bible*.

People often feel that if a company is not listed at their career center, or in one of the directories we've just mentioned, that the company has no interest in hiring an intern or volunteer, but this is not necessarily the case. If you don't see the name of the company you most want to work for in one of these books, feel free to call them up and offer your services. It is kind of flattering to a company to know that a bright articulate person (we are referring to you, of course) wants to work for them so badly that he or she is willing to do so for free. Write a Great Letter (see chapter 5) and watch your mailbox.

WHAT ARE EMPLOYERS LOOKING FOR IN AN INTERN?

Experience. Okay, don't curse like that. This isn't our fault. Of *course* we know that the whole reason you want an internship is to *get* experience. And how, you may well ask, can employers expect you to have experience *before* they hire you?

It turns out that you already have quite a lot of

Best-paid women in corporate America

Rena Rowan
Executive VP, Jones Apparel

$4,003,000

Sherry Lansing
Chairman, Paramount Pictures

$3,000,000

Carol Bartz
CEO, Autodesk

$2,570,000

Linda Wachner
President, CEO, Warnaco

$2,360,000

Jill E. Barad
President, Mattel USA

$1,375,211

Marion Sandler
Co-CEO, Golden West Financial

$2,030,000

(Source: Working Woman, January 1995)

experience; you just have to learn to look at it the right way. In chapter 5, you will find lots of hints on how to put your summer jobs, extracurricular activities, and academic responsibilities in the best light.

ARE GRADES IMPORTANT?

For some types of internships, grades can be very important. According to the director of the internship program at Columbia University, "The standards in different fields tend to be the same for internships as they are for jobs. Engineering companies and financial institutions look for a high GPA, while museums, for example, are more likely to be interested in the courses you've taken and your expertise in the field."

HOW TO APPLY

The process of applying for an internship or a volunteer job is not unlike that of applying for a job. Some internships are hotly sought after, so be sure to apply for more than one. WNET, a public television station in New York, received 1,000 applications for 35 positions last year.

If you are interested in a summer internship, the best time to apply is usually between December and March, but individual companies may have their own ideas about deadlines, so read the listings carefully. There are no formal deadlines for term-long internships. Companies hire these interns throughout the year.

Each listing, whether you found it in a directory or on a bulletin board at school, will contain a contact name. This is the person who is in charge of hiring interns or volunteers. To apply for an internship, send your resume and a cover letter to the contact person. (Resumes and cover letters are so important that we have devoted an entire chapter to them later on in this book.)

Two weeks later, you should follow up with a polite phone call. Ask to speak to the person to whom you wrote your letter. Don't be upset if he can't come to the phone the first time you call. A personnel director once confided to Lanna Hagge, the director of Career

Shannon Hudnall had been doing a part-time internship at a government agency during her senior year at Georgetown in Washington, D.C. "It was just supposed to be a filing and fetching coffee sort of job, but I decided to really go for it—so I did a lot of things that weren't part of the job description." The result? Shannon made a great impression and was offered a temporary job after she graduated.

"So then I happened to be talking on the telephone with a man from an international trade consulting firm who I'd dealt with during my internship. I knew he thought I'd done well at the internship, so I asked him if he had heard of any jobs, since all I had was a temporary job. He called back in two minutes, and said yes, he did know of a job. I'm starting this Monday."

Services at Oberlin, that "I never return the first phone call, but I always return the second." Obviously, this guy likes to see how serious his job candidates are. Not all employers will refuse your phone call out of gamesmanship. They may simply be too busy at the moment you called. Try them again, and don't take a "Sorry, Ms. Nelson is on another line" personally.

When you call, it is a good idea for you to have some questions written down in front of you, in case you get through. "Is there any other information you need?" "Would you like me to call you next week?" Sometimes, your contact person may have time to chat, in which case you may find yourself being interviewed right then and there over the telephone.

However, most of the time, the next step in the process, if an employer is interested in you, is an in-person interview.

THE INTERVIEW

An interview for an internship or a volunteer job will be much like an interview for a regular job. Chapter 9 is devoted to this subject, but there are a few pointers that should be mentioned now.

As with any interview, you want to walk into the room knowing as much as possible about your prospective employer. If you found out about this job through your college career center, the center will almost certainly have a folder of information on the company. Read everything they have, but remember that everyone else who applies for this position from your school has probably read the same folder. If you really want to impress your interviewer, take it a step further. Go to the public library. See if there have been any recent newspaper or magazine articles written about the company. If they have just put out a new candy bar, take the time to try one. If they have just put out a new movie, take the time to go see it.

Because internships are less defined than real jobs, it helps to try to find out as much as possible about what you can expect and what will be expected of you. Ask lots of questions about what your specific duties will be.

Top 10 job markets in the U.S.

1. Washington, D.C.
2. Anaheim, CA
3. Atlanta, GA
4. Phoenix, AZ
5. San Diego, CA
6. Tampa/St. Petersburg, FL
7. Orlando, FL
8. Dallas, TX
9. Riverside, CA
10. Minneapolis/ St. Paul, MN

(Source: Money Magazine, 1995)

Of course, what you're trying to find out is whether this is just a busywork sort of job, or if there are genuine chances to learn and take on responsibility. This may be hard to tell in advance, both for you *and* the employer, because he doesn't know yet what you're capable of. Internships and volunteer jobs are often what you make of them. If you go in there and blow them away with your zeal and initiative, you may end up running the place. Or you may alienate everyone there.

If the internship is supposed to earn you college credit, pin down exactly how many hours you will be working and then check with your school to make sure you will accrue enough hours to qualify.

If the person interviewing you is not the person you would be working under, try to meet your potential boss so you can get a sense of whether this is a person you would enjoy working with.

Don't be disheartened if you are not offered the job on the spot. Most employers will want to see all the available candidates before they make a decision.

AFTER THE INTERVIEW

No matter how ambivalent they may have been about the job before they applied, most people find themselves secretly hoping to get an offer. When they get the phone call, they are often so ecstatic that they accept on the spot. There is nothing wrong with a little euphoria, but remember to say no if the job does not suit you.

Take some time right after the interview to think about what you learned while you were there. What was the work environment like in the office? Was it fast paced, or mellow, and did that suit your temperament? Did the other employees seem to enjoy being there? Did you get the sense that your prospective boss would allow you some real responsibility if you showed that you could handle it?

Now (even if you've decided you would not take this internship if it were the last job on earth) sit down and write a thank-you note, and put it in the mail. The pool of possible employers is not infinite. You may want to work for this company sometime down the road.

The Job Itself

It's not hard to see why companies love the concept of an internship—where else are they going to get an inexhaustible supply of bright, hardworking young college graduates who are willing to work like dogs for little or no money. But remember, you are getting something valuable as well: the experience you need for your resume, the opportunity to see what a particular field is really like, and a chance to shine.

This may be your first exposure to the work environment, and inevitably you will find yourself wondering how such an inefficient organization could ever stay in business. Keep these thoughts to yourself. You will be partly right, but only partly. No organization functions at peak efficiency 365 days a year. Remember also that you are seeing only a small part of the picture. After the first week, you may have decided that all your boss does all day is talk on the phone. By the end of the internship you will have realized that she is still at her desk three hours after you have left, doing the paperwork she didn't have time to get to during the day.

You will probably also have realized that offices break down into two philosophical camps: the "this is just what I do for a living" group, and the "I'm staying until this is done perfectly" group. We wouldn't dream of telling you which group to join, but we *will* point out that it is the second group of exciting young women and men who become celebrated, rich, and powerful.

Try to find someone at your workplace who you admire. Watch how this person deals with the other people in the office. How does he handle a tough situation? If possible, try to become friends.

No matter how great the internship, there will always be some routine, boring tasks for you to do, so don't whine about them. Volunteer for more interesting tasks *in addition to* the boring tasks. Perhaps you can make yourself so valuable that they will not want to waste you on photocopying. If your boss is not telling you how you're doing, make sure to ask. Some bosses are not good at communicating their feelings, good or bad. Ask yourself whether you are meeting the goals that have been set for you. When the internship is over, write a very appreciative thank-you letter.

Corning makes 81% of its job offers to former interns.

(Source: Money Magazine, 1994)

If you really hit it off with your boss, get a letter of recommendation while the experience is still fresh in her mind and then keep in contact. A postcard or a phone call every once in a while to ask how things are going will help to make that boss a permanent part of your network, someone you can call for advice and help for years to come.

A Summer, a January, a Term, a Year?

How long should you spend in an internship or volunteer job? Each time period has its advantages.

Committing to a year or a term can be tough if you are still in school. You may lose out on some important fringe benefits of campus life—we're speaking here not just of friendships but of on-campus extracurricular activities that can also be important for your resume. On the other hand, a solid block of time on the job can lead to real experience, real responsibility, and a chance to shine.

The advantages of a summer or January internship are self-apparent; they are relatively short so you have a chance to try several related fields, or even several different fields in quick succession. You also have the chance to make a nice, sharp, short impression and then get out before they get tired of you. Short internships or volunteer jobs are also less expensive and less disruptive of your school experience.

Starting Early Later

If you are supporting yourself during an internship, employers are often willing to adjust your internship schedule to accommodate your "money gig." Employers, like everyone, admire fortitude. If you're working three nights a week in order to be able to afford to keep your internship, they will often go out of their way to rearrange the total number of internship hours.

Cooperative Education

Cooperative education is a program available at over nine hundred colleges in the United States that lets you combine a college education with a job in your intended field. Generally, students spend alternate terms attending classes full time and then working full time at off-campus jobs with private companies.

The big attraction here is that cooperative ed jobs are almost always paid—sometimes *well* paid. Students earn money for tuition while getting practical on-the-job experience in their areas of interest. After graduating, a high percentage of cooperative education students get hired permanently by the companies they worked for during school. Companies from every conceivable field participate in this program. The federal government is the largest employer of cooperative education students.

Students generally join a cooperative education program in their junior or senior year. After you are accepted, you get assigned a counselor, and the two of you sit down with a huge list of jobs, and window-shop. You apply for the job or jobs, you are interested in. It is up to the employers whether you get hired.

Cooperative education can be particularly useful if you are a communications major. Internships at newspapers and television stations are virtually never salaried. However, some colleges that sponsor cooperative education have created hybrid salaried internships that are paid for with college funds. It is also sometimes possible, if your prospective employer is a nonprofit company, to receive work-study funds for a cooperative education job.

Getting a degree through the cooperative education program generally takes about five years, but the students who emerge from this program have a huge head-start over their classmates; they already have valuable experience and a prospective employer in their field. They owe less money in student loans, and they are often paid a higher starting salary than new hirees.

THE INTERNSHIP AS PRACTICE

Even if an internship weren't such a valuable way to explore and gain work experience, you could argue that it was worth it just for the practice it provides for your real job hunt to come. Each step along the way—deciding who you want to work for, putting together a resume, interviewing, fielding offers, and then finally working in an area you are interested in—mirrors the real job-hunting process that is to come.

But to illustrate the very best features of internships, we'll let a statistic speak for itself: AT&T says it ends up hiring 50% of its former interns for permanent positions.

How to Find a Job (almost) Without Leaving Campus: Your College's Job Placement Center

We know. You always *meant* to visit the job placement center at your school, but you somehow never got around to it. It was on the other side of campus, you were busy writing papers, you had to wash your hair.

If you're still in school or if you're a relatively recent graduate, there are six excellent reasons to make a beeline straight for your placement center: the recruitment program, the classes in resume writing, the videotaped mock interviews, the extensive library of career-related books, the information on internships, and the vocational testing.

But the best reason of all is the simplest: believe it or not, there are several people sitting in that suite of offices you never quite got around to visiting who are actually paid by the university to help find you a job.

Is This a Great Country or What?

Unlike commercial employment agencies that have a vested interest in getting you to take a job—any job—as soon as possible, your college career placement service has almost no ax to grind. It is extremely unlikely that you will ever hear an employment agency person tell you, "Take your time. Do more research. Don't let me rush you into anything." Commercial employment agencies need warm bodies to fill vacant positions, and they don't get paid until they fill them. By contrast, your college placement counselor wants you to be happy.

"We start by getting the students to look at their own values," says Machiek Kolodziejczab (that's his name), a career counselor at the UCLA Placement and Career Planning Center. "We're not here to put them on the fast track. Our job is to enable and empower them. Learning how to write a resume and interview are not one-time-only events. We see these as *life skills*."

Okay, he's from California, but this is actually the way *all* college placement people talk. The advice you get from a college job placement counselor is a curious mixture of the pragmatic and the ephemeral. On the one hand, you can't get more pragmatic than finding a job to put food on the table. On the other hand, college job placement counselors are willing to talk to you for hours—well, at least 45 minutes during a scheduled appointment—about such ephemeral matters as the quality of your life, what kind of moral values are acceptable to you in the workplace, and whether that necktie goes with that shirt.

"It isn't realistic to expect students to know right away what they're going to do for the rest of their lives," says Eileen Kohn, the head of the Columbia University Center for Career Services. "They need to kick around ideas; to explore."

Internships

Naturally, college counselors hope that you start exploring *before* May of your senior year. "Where it breaks down for a lot of graduates is when they don't know what they want to do," says Lanna Hagge, the head of Oberlin College's Career Services Center. "They say they'll do anything, but they don't really mean it."

Nicole Poses's job search began with a visit to the job placement center at her college. She was in her senior year at Syracuse, and knew she wanted to get into marketing, specifically, at a cosmetics firm.

She was going through the list of companies that would be recruiting at Syracuse that spring when she saw a listing for Estée Lauder; unfortunately, the listing said they were looking only for engineers. "I made friends with the head recruiter in New York, called him every day, and annoyed him until he agreed to give me an interview. I didn't think I'd get a second interview since I wasn't an engineer, but they called me a couple of weeks later and flew me down to New York City to interview for a marketing job. I thought it went horribly, and I cried when I left, because I really wanted the job and I was sure I didn't get it—and then I got it."

The best way to explore what you want to do, as we've said already, is to start the process early (as we advised in chapter 3). Summer internships and volunteer jobs not only give you credibility with future employers but also allow you to get a feel for a particular industry or field.

There is no better place to find an internship than at a college. These days, thousands of companies are actively looking for interns. What better place to look than college campuses? Your placement office will have lists of companies that are particularly interested in applicants from your school (perhaps the head of the company is an alumnus, or perhaps they've simply had good luck in the past with students from your school).

Your placement center personnel also talk to last year's interns, so they are in a good position to tell you which internships have been the most interesting and the most fruitful for former students.

The placement office will also have the latest copies of books like The Princeton Review's *Student Access Guide to America's Top Internships* and *Student Access Guide: The Internship Bible*, as well as information on the cooperative education programs we discussed in chapter 3.

Most common causes of death in the workplace	
	% of all worker deaths
Assaults	21%
Highway accidents	20%
Falls	10%
Caught in, under, between objects	10%
Struck by objects	9%
Electrocutions	5%
Airplane Crashes	4%
Explosions	3%

(Monthly Labor Review, 1994)

VOCATIONAL TESTING

Another way students can explore their options is to take vocational skills tests such as the Strong-Campbell Interest Inventory, or the Meyers-Briggs Test. These tests, available at most placement centers, are designed to help give you some insights into what kind of a career might make you happy. After you take the test, it is sent away to be scored (cost to you: under $10), and several weeks later, you sit down with a counselor to discuss the results. "There are never any surprises," says Mary Giannini, a former career counselor. "Students already know in a vague way what they're good at. They come in looking for a real specific answer like, 'You should be a chemical engineer specializing in synthetic petroleum'; the answers are much vaguer than that. A test like this is simply an instrument to open up a dialogue." The most important part of a vocational test is talking about the results afterward. Your counselor may be able to look at your skills with a more dispassionate eye than you have right now (certainly with a more dispassionate eye than your parents have).

COMPUTER COUNSELING

While many colleges now routinely use internet links to provide students with up-to-the-minute databases of hundreds of thousands of potential jobs and employers, some colleges are taking computer technology even further: a few schools have begun using software programs such as *Discover, Career Design,* and *Career Navigator,* all of which are designed to, well, if not replace, then at least augment a human counselor. The programs take you through a series of exercises to help you figure out what you are good at, and build up your confidence.

RESUME WRITING AND MOCK INTERVIEWS

Once you have an idea of what kind of job you want, you'll have to put together a resume and practice your interviewing skills. Many college career centers hold regular workshops in both these areas. You may find that your interviewing class will include several videotaped mock interviews. You can go home later and watch yourself again and again as you sit back suavely in your best suit and say, "I'm glad you asked me that, Glen. My worst attribute is that I'm too conscientious."

We are issuing you this plea on behalf of your future children: *please,* don't throw away that video.

THE RECRUITMENT PROGRAM

For generations, the early fall and late winter of senior year have meant putting on your one decent dress or suit, borrowing a pair of shoes, and going to the on-campus recruitment interviews set up by large corporations. In your parents' time, these interviews were relatively easy to come by, as companies flocked to colleges, paying for the privilege of getting an early look at the year's crop of graduates.

These days, things have changed quite a bit. As Eileen Kohn from Columbia says, "These programs are becoming

Toughest interview question

"So, tell us your worst attribute."

dinosaurs. Companies are beginning to realize that they can get to the students they want through the internet."

Small colleges and colleges located off the beaten path have seen on-campus recruitment drop significantly. To counter this trend many small colleges have banded together to pool their job-hunting resources. The Selected Liberal Arts Consortium (which includes Oberlin) is one of these groups. It is made up of seven colleges that jointly sponsor job fairs for their students in major cities across America. "The idea is that if the corporations can't come to our students, we send our students to see them," says Hagge, of Oberlin. Corporations receive resumes of students interested in being interviewed. The corporations "prescreen" the resumes—meaning they decide which students they actually want to see—and then those students travel to Boston, New York, Washington, D.C., Los Angeles, San Francisco, Philadelphia, or Chicago for their recruitment interviews, often held in hotels or convention centers.

How Recruitment Prescreening Works

Whether you are trying for a recruitment interview on or off campus, you will probably have to submit resumes for "prescreening."

What are the companies looking for in the prescreening?

They are looking for reasons *not* to see you. For one thing, recruiting teams don't have unlimited time and they want to cut down the number of students they have to see. For another, it is much easier to reject a resume than it is to reject a person with a face and a story.

Therefore, they would like to see typos on your resume. They want to see messy graphics. They want to see a confusing or meandering layout. They want to see grammatical mistakes. Give them what they want—and you will never get to look at the inside of one of those little cubicles.

So you have to give them what they don't want: a well-organized, spell-checked, error-free resume, flawlessly printed on white paper. For much more detail, refer to chapter 5.

Josh Margulies was looking through the job listings at the Columbia College job placement office, and came upon a listing that he decided must have gotten there by mistake. "It said, 'investigator for the investigative arm of the state legislature; power to subpoena, power to swear witnesses.' I looked at that and said to myself, 'they've got to be kidding.' I mean, I'm only 21 years old. I was the only Columbia grad who was crazy enough to even apply."

The listing didn't say who was actually doing the hiring, but Josh went to the library, and found out everything he could about the state senator who chaired the committee. "I knew who the guy was, I knew the name of his dog...."

Josh also decided that a personal connection couldn't hurt. "It was really funny, but I found out that the senator who chairs the committee is the county chair for the party, and naturally, he knows all the county chairs from around the state. And I happened to have delivered newspapers for the former county chair from my hometown. So my Mom called him, and he wrote me a great recommendation."

When Josh got to the interview, it was the state senator himself who was doing the interviewing. "He asked me about my family, and I told him that my sister had graduated with honors from Harvard, *too*. He said, 'Oh, did you go to Harvard?' and I said, 'No, sir. You did.'" The rest, as they say, is history.

How Important Are Grades?

Number of billionaires in America	
1987	49
1988	51
1989	67
1990	66
1991	71

(Forbes, 1991)

Some companies, particularly financial companies, will ask to see only applicants with high GPAs. However, there are two things to understand here.

First, this is sometimes just another convenient way to cut down the number of people they have to see rather than an immutable standard to which they hold all new employees. In other words, you may be able to find ways to make them ignore your grades (more on this later).

Second, though a high GPA will get you in the door, it won't get you the job all by itself. "Every year, we get a couple of 3.9s who come in distraught because a 3.2 got the job," says Kolodziejczab of UCLA. "Good grades give you options, but employers want healthy, balanced people." When someone emerges, pale and squinting in the light, from four years spent studying nonstop in the library, it may cause even an accounting firm to wonder what this person would be like at the Christmas party.

The good news is that once you have actually gotten in the door to see them, recruiters want to like you. Recruiting teams take pride in how many people they end up placing at their company. They will be rooting for you back at the company headquarters. Best of all, the recruiting teams sent by the corporations are often not made up of hardened personnel-types. Many recruiters are volunteers from the corporation, sometimes only a few years out of school themselves—and it's not out of the question that the school they came from might be your own.

A Guaranteed Method to Find Something in Common with Your Interviewer

You go in to meet a potential employer, your antennae quivering for some common interest that will make him decide to be your mentor for life. After several banal exchanges, you finally elicit from him that he is a lover of fourteenth-century Tibetan pottery. Some friendly advice: no matter how long it has been since you have last eaten, do NOT say,

"Oh, really? I, also, happen to be a lover of fourteenth-century Tibetan pottery."

For one thing, since you probably aren't a lover of fourteenth-century Tibetan pottery, and since he probably really is, you can't hope to carry off this imposture for more than a few seconds.

The odds of going into an interview with a stranger and discovering that you share a real common interest are fairly small.

However, when your interviewer is an alum, you already know you have something in common: you went to the same school. This may not seem like much of a connection to you—but trust us, it's a big connection for your prospective mentor. A mysterious chemical process takes place shortly after graduation, causing all alumni to turn into mush when they hear the old school song. You will find that you can make him mist up merely by throwing out the names of decrepit buildings on campus.

> You: *"Remember that old tool shed behind the library?"*

> Alum: *"Oh, the* tool shed. *Is that still there?"*

This will be pretty much true regardless of where you both went to school. Even an alum of a huge place like the University of Michigan (with a current student population of 21,971) will still feel a bond with a young U. of Michigan graduate—particularly if you encounter her in another state. In a recruitment interview, your chances of getting an alumnus are pretty much hit or miss. However, recruitment interviews are not the only way to meet an alum.

ALUMNI MENTOR PROGRAMS

There may be a few college grads out there who don't undergo that weird chemical process, but if there are they certainly didn't sign up to be part of the alumni mentor program at your school. Most colleges make some kind of effort to help current graduates connect with older graduates. These efforts can range from informal steering ("Why don't you call a friend of mine in . . .") to formal programs that are designed to pair students

Deborah Novick went to visit the job placement office at the University of Pennsylvania often during the year she was a senior. "I kept dropping my resume in the drop slots for different recruitment interviews." She was eventually selected to interview for Macy's. "At the interview, the guy was reading my resume, and he said, 'Echo Lake. You're an Echo Laker?' We had both worked as camp counselors at the same camp. Then he said, 'Novick . . . that sounds familiar.' And at the same time we both said 'Bob.' It turned out he had been my brother's camp counselor."

"He said, 'I'll make sure I get you to New York, but don't let me down.'" The second interviewer did not turn out to be from her kindergarten class or anything like that, but Deborah apparently did pretty well anyway, because she was hired immediately and has worked there ever since.

up with alums who are already working in their field of interest.

At many schools the placement services keep large binders full of the names of alumni who have agreed to talk to students. The binders are organized by profession, and updated frequently. If you were interested in working for a mutual fund, for example, you could look in the "finance" binder, and find several alums of different ages, all of whom work in the mutual fund industry. Each has written a brief description of what he or she does, and what it's like working in that field. If you are interested, you can set up an "informational interview."

ARE THEY BREATHING? GOOD. CALL THEM.

At Oberlin, working on the theory that "*every* alumnus wants to help new graduates," the career center has computer printouts, by location and by profession, of every alumnus still on this earth. In addition, during their annual job-a-thon, the center calls thousands of alumni and parents for information about possible openings. Last year the job-a-thon produced over a thousand leads for a class of seven hundred.

Most colleges in America have printouts like these, and encourage their graduates, new and old, to make use of them. In a few years, when it's time to look for your second job, you can come back and look up your former classmates. Perhaps it will turn out that someone from your old dorm is working at the very company you're interested in.

WHAT IF MY SCHOOL DOESN'T HAVE ALUMNI PRINTOUTS?

If your college is one of the few that don't provide these printouts at the job center, find out who is in charge of the alumni association (believe us, even if it doesn't have an alumni mentor program, every college has an alumni association—how else do they raise money for the new library?). The alumni association will have current addresses for anyone who contributes regularly (a good indication that they feel warmly toward the old school),

Louis Fabregas got his degree from the University of Bridgeport. "I went on a few campus interviews, but I wasn't offered anything I really wanted to do." Louis was after a job in financial analysis, "and I knew the big six were expanding and diversifying." After he graduated he went to his school's alumnae association, who gave him the name of one of the partners at Andersen, a financial consulting firm. "So I sent him a cover letter with my resume. Actually, I never spoke to that partner, but I guess he liked my cover letter and resume and he passed them on to his assistant. The first interview was with a recruiter, but then a month later, I met with four managers and a partner, and then had lunch with some of the senior staffers from the group. I went on a few other interviews during this process, but this was the job I wanted."

and will probably have some information about alums' occupations as well. Reading the alumni newsletter or magazine will also help you track down people in your prospective field, as well as tell you interesting trivia about them.

An Underutilized Resource

You might think that these people would be swamped with students wanting informational interviews, but according to Eileen Kohn, head of Columbia's placement program (and this was echoed by employees at other college placement programs with mentor programs) this is not the case at all. "We have hundreds of alumni on file, and many of them never get a call."

It may feel a bit strange to call a stranger on the telephone and ask her for a meeting. It is much easier just to send out a hundred resumes that will probably get tossed in the garbage, unread. However, if you really want a job, you are eventually going to have to see someone in person. Just keep reminding yourself: these people already like you. You went to their school.

Cyber College

Many colleges have joined the 21st century by putting up web sites on the internet—and their career centers have generally followed suit with offerings of their own. These can range from a few token downloadable brochures, to extensive job listings with hypertext links to the home pages of the potential employers. There is nothing more painless than finding a job listing, signing up for an interview for the job, and then researching the company—all without leaving your dorm room. For more on using the internet, see chapter 7.

How to Get Your Placement Office to Give You Its Best

When you ask placement counselors and staff about the students they remember best, their faces light up and they describe students from as long ago as five years as if it had all happened last week. "There was this one guy," recalls a counselor from a school in the Northeast.

"Frank Wilson ('73) writes that he loves his job as head of marketing at TLP, and adds that he has recently taken up bowling."

(Source: Alumnae Magazine of Anywhere University)

Interview with Career Center Librarian Dorothy London

"Have you ever been asked for information about a particular career and you didn't have any?"

"No."

"OK, say I want a career in whaling in Japan?"

"I would discourage you from that field," she says, severely.

I just stand in front of her, silently waiting.

"Well," she offers finally, *"I do have a listing of Japanese maritime associations you could write to."*

"He was a nice guy, with lots of extracurricular activities, and he wanted a job in banking, but his grades were only average. He kept getting close, but not getting the job. So I helped him meet some people. Not only did he get a job but he's also been promoted twice in three years."

Obviously, this counselor went the extra mile for that student and felt personally connected enough to want to know what was happening in his career two years later. What makes a counselor go the extra mile? When asked, counselors respond almost guiltily, as if there were something less than fair about giving some students more attention than others. However, when it came down to it, they all had suggestions for ways to win their hearts.

DON'T JUST SHOW UP SENIOR YEAR

"It's easier when they come in a lot to use the facilities," says one career service staff member at NYU. "We get to know them as people. We get to see them grow up and change."

By giving the people at your career services center time to get to know you, you will also give them time to develop a personal stake in your success. Take the trouble to find out about *them*. Where did *they* go to school? What were their first jobs out of college? What are the names of their children?

Of course, it's useless to pretend an interest that you don't feel. If you don't connect with a particular person, don't try to fake it. Unless you are a scoundrel, you will not be very convincing anyway. Be polite and courteous, and then find another counselor or staff member with whom you *do* connect.

If you are reading this as a junior in college, re-member that you should be in there visiting right now: the college placement center is the best place to start looking for a summer internship or for information about cooperative education. Even if financial circumstances make it necessary for you to work at a less exotic but higher paying job this summer, you should come in to the center anyway and explain why you aren't looking for an internship. College placement staff members work

Fastest-growing professions	
increase by year 2005	
Paralegal	85%
Systems analyst	79%
Physical therapist	76%
Psychologist	64%
Travel agent	62%
Correction officer	61%
Flight attendant	60%
Computer programmer	56%
Management analyst	52%
Marketing/P.R.	47%
Doctor	34%
Lawyer	34%

(Source: Bureau of Labor Statistics, 1993)

for a living themselves, and they will be impressed by your dedication to paying for college.

Students who are participating in the work-study program at school can often request particular assignments. If you are in the work-study program, it would not be a ridiculous idea for you to request an assignment in your career services center. Working in the cafeteria may give you valuable insights into steam tray cooking, but a job in career services can get you a head start on your career.

If you are reading this two weeks before graduation, or even during the two years after graduation, don't panic. As we said earlier, whenever you start the job-hunting process is when you start. Tell your counselor that you realize a job hunt takes some time, and that you are interested in beginning now. He will be impressed with your poise and your realistic attitude.

BE *POLITELY* AGGRESSIVE

"Seek it out, and be persistent," said Kolodziejczab at UCLA. "In our office, it usually takes a month to set up an interview, because we're so busy. But every year a few students just come knock on my door. What can I say? I reward that kind of behavior."

At large schools, students are often listed on the school computer by social security number rather than by name. Especially at these larger schools, it is easy to get lost in the bureaucratic shuffle. Students who know what they want and go after it tend to get better results. The sooner you can establish some kind of relationship with one of the counselors, the sooner you stop being an anonymous social security number. Your determination in getting in to see your counselor will also show him your determination to do well in the interviews he sets up for you.

Of course, there is a fine line between being politely aggressive and being a jerk. If your counselor calls campus security, you have probably crossed that line.

Resume blunders

Robert Half, head of Accountemps, counsels clients on their resumes. Here are excerpts from some first drafts presented to him over the years:

Grilled free-range deductions:

"Duties: Senior accountant, prepared journal entrees for companies."

And his memory is real good too:

"Excellent memory; strong math aptitude; excellent memory; effective management skills; and very good at math."

But you can't make her think:

"My experience in horticulture is well-rooted."

(Source: Accountemps)

Live up to Your Commitments

"*Some* students are finding jobs easily, and you might ask why," said a staff member at Columbia. "I think those are the same students who show up on time for their appointments with us, who do their homework before recruitment interviews, who participate in our programs."

Before a career service staffer is going to go out of her way for you, she needs to know that you are going to justify her faith in you. If you miss appointments, miss deadlines, or start singing "My Way" during your interview, she is not likely to try real hard in the future.

Placement counselors and staff are just like anyone else. They want to feel useful in their jobs, and they like to help people who appreciate the help they receive. To get them to do their best, approach them the same way you would approach a prospective employer. Don't act like you're entitled to their help. Be grateful. Write thank-you notes. When something goes well, remember to share your triumph with them.

And stay in touch. After all, you may need to come back in a year or two.

You Can Go Home Again

Most college job placement centers allow alumni of any age to use at least some of their services. Recruitment programs are usually only for graduating seniors, but often you will be able to use the library facilities, arrange for an appointment with a counselor, consult computer listings of alumni, and look over the job boards, even if you have been out of college for years.

This can be especially handy if you decide to take a year off instead of plunging immediately into the work world (a topic we'll cover in chapter 14). After backpacking through the Himalayas for a year, you may feel a little out of practice in your interviewing skills.

You should recognize, however, that you will no longer be the career services staff's top priority—after all, they have an entire graduating class to take care of. However, if you took the time to cultivate them when you were there the first time, they will be pleased to see you.

"Those who seek mentoring will rule the great expanse under heaven."

(Shu Ching, *Chinese Book of History*, circa sixth century B.C.)

This is really no different from the networking you are going to be doing in your job. You never know when someone from your past is going to be able to do you a favor. By taking the time to get to know the people with whom you come into contact, and ensuring that you leave them with a good impression, you sow the seeds for all kinds of wonderful opportunities in the future.

Another possible option if you have been out of school for a while is the university clubs found in large cities. Some of these clubs run career counseling programs and workshops for their members. Of course, to take advantage of these services, you would have to be a member of the club.

ONE SMALL WARNING ABOUT YOUR COLLEGE CAREER COUNSELORS

While job placement staff at your college are not paid on the basis of how many students they place, their performance is ultimately going to be *measured* by the number of students they place. You may find that if you are actually offered a job as a result of their efforts, the center personnel may nudge you kind of hard to accept it.

And while it is great if you can involve your career counselor in your career, it is sometimes possible for your counselor to get too involved. Once you stir maternal or paternal instincts, your counselor may start wanting for you the same thing your parents want for you—nothing less than total financial and emotional security *right now*. Since this may or may not be what you have in mind for your immediate future, you should be prepared to take your counselor's concern with a grain of salt.

There is ultimately only one person who can decide whether a job is right for you; don't let anyone pressure you into taking a job you don't want.

IF YOUR COLLEGE'S CAREER CENTER IS NO GOOD OR NONEXISTENT

Not every school has a great placement program, and not every career center welcomes alumni. If you are unable or unwilling to use your school's career center, you will find that many of the same services are available elsewhere if you look for them. Most cities have at least one public library with a decent section on careers. Here you will discover many of the same books and directories you would find at a good college career center library.

For a more personal touch, classes in resume writing and interviewing are often available through adult education classes at your community college for little or no money. A potential drawback to these courses is that the professional level of the other people taking the course may not be the same as your own. It's a good idea to check out ahead of time the credentials of both the person teaching the course and the other students who are taking it.

If you feel you need a career counselor, you can either go to a regular employment agency where there will probably be no fee or you can hire a career counselor at an hourly rate (see chapter 8, "Employment Agencies, Career Counselors, and Head Hunters").

If you no longer live close enough to visit your alma mater, it may be possible to use the facilities at another college. Some schools have reciprocal arrangements whereby their students are allowed to use each other's job centers. In some cases, you may find that the facilities are better at the reciprocal-agreement college than they are at your own.

And for what it's worth, only two of the five career centers we visited while researching this chapter asked us for identification when we visited their libraries.

Tools to Get Employers to See You: The Resume, the Great Letter, Using the New Technologies

THE RESUME

You wouldn't think that anything so straightforward could inspire such passionate debate, but in fact career counselors, personnel experts, and human resources people all sharply disagree with each other about the purpose and meaning of the resume. Some see it as "an extended calling card" or "marketing tool" that should be sent out into the world in huge numbers, sort of like pollen, to spread and take root in likely places. Others feel a resume should never be the first contact between an employer and a candidate—that its only purpose is to confirm an employer's good opinion *after* a first meeting arranged through networking.

However, pretty much all the experts agree on one thing: you have to have one. There is no way around it; no matter how novel and original your job search, at some point someone is going to say, "You sound very interesting. Let me see your resume."

Writing a resume can be an emotionally trying experience. Somehow, seeing your life reduced to a page of harsh text brings out almost everyone's insecurities. "Why don't I have more accomplishments?" people demand of themselves. "Why didn't I study for that biology exam instead of going to Fort Lauderdale?" You should remind yourself that if you don't yet have many accomplishments it is partly because of your number one strength: you are brand new. Employers will be hiring you for your newness, not your oldness. And if your grades are less than outstanding, you should realize that this first job hunt is probably the last time anyone is going to care about your academic record. After this, you will be judged on what you've accomplished in the real world.

A RESUME'S APPEARANCE

Even though the experts disagree as to what a resume is good for, they all agree about what it should look like: first and foremost, there can be NO TYPOS. Many employers use resumes as a way to reduce the number of people they will have to see in person. Thus any spelling or grammatical error will be an excuse to toss your resume into the wastepaper basket. Your resume must be perfectly typed, preferably laser printed, on plain good-quality white paper. If at all possible, the paper stock and printing font should match those of your cover letter. The design of the resume is critical; it should have clean lines without too many different fonts, indentations, or other visually distracting features, and it should fit on a single page. Finally, with the easy availability of desktop publishing, it also makes sense to write your resume on a computer, so you can update it frequently or even tailor it toward specific jobs as they come up.

THE THREE PARTS OF A RESUME

A resume has three main sections: education, work experience, and activities. There are several other categories you may want to add as well, depending on your personal situation: skills, languages, travel, personal background. All these sections can be arranged in different orders, depending on how long you have been out of school and what you are trying to accomplish with the resume. However, if you are a recent graduate you will want to put the education section first, since it is almost certainly, up to now at least, your greatest accomplishment. We're going to describe each of the elements of the

Mike Jordan spent his first three years of college at the London School of Economics. He spent his senior year at Drew University, keeping up a full course load while working four days a week selling insurance for the Equitable. "My boss at the Equitable was fired. They offered me a full-time job, but the salary was lower than what I'd been making while I was still in college."

He put 150 resumes in a briefcase and went to New York City. "It was just an instinct. I went to the financial district, and midtown, and went into office buildings that looked likely, picked names from the directories, took the elevator upstairs, and just walked in."

He dropped off over one hundred resumes. "I went in like a salesman: 'Hi, my name is Mike Jordan.'" One of the companies he visited was Showtime, the cable television network. They called him in for an interview, and hired him to work in their accounting department.

resume briefly, and then take you through a couple of case studies so you can see how the different elements go together.

EDUCATION

Schools should be listed in reverse chronological order, starting with the school you most recently attended (or are attending) and working backward. Include the college, its location, the dates you attended the school, the date you received (or will receive) your degree, your major, your GPA (if above 3.2), honors, and awards if any. Then you may want to throw in educational experiences that tie in with the job you're applying for. If your senior thesis is even marginally related, you should describe it briefly. You should be aware, however, that among other things, the resume is a list of possible conversation topics for your interview, so if you list your thesis on your resume, you should be prepared to talk about it fervently, on demand. You could include language proficiency or other skills here or break them out into their own section later on. If you attended another college previously, repeat the process we've just described for that college as well.

Should you include high school? The answer is no, with a couple exceptions. If you attended a prestigious prep school that is very likely to be recognized by your potential employer, it makes sense to mention it. If you attended a specialized high school for the arts or a certain trade—and you're pursuing a career in the area you specialized in—include your high school on your resume. Otherwise, drop it. Once you've been out of college for a few years, and have more experience, your high school experience will become less relevant, and you can drop it from the resume. But until then, every job counts.

WORK EXPERIENCE

There are a number of different formats you can use to describe your work experience. We'll be showing you several options in our case studies, but for the most part, new graduates are expected to list work experience in reverse chronological order.

Number of Job Openings for College Graduates in 1990:

964,000

Number of New Graduates in 1990:

974,000

Number of Old Graduates Seeking Jobs in 1990:

214,000

Projected Number of Job Openings for College Graduates in 2005:

914,000

Projected Number of New Graduates in 2005:

1,106,000

Projected Number of Old Graduates Seeking Jobs in 2005:

214,000

(Source: Monthly Labor Review, July 1992)

The work experience section covers a lot of territory. It should include all the work you're proud of—real jobs or internships, paid or unpaid—even if the experience was relatively brief. Face it, at this point your *life* has been fairly brief. The way you describe these experiences will to some degree be dictated by the particular jobs you are applying for (about which we will be going into in more detail shortly). However, certain items must always be there: the job title, the organization you worked for, its location, and the dates you worked there. You can put these in any order that makes your experience sound the most impressive, but you must be consistent.

> United States Congress, Washington, D.C.
> —intern, summer of 1991
>
> Ed's Auto Supply, Southold, NY
> —assistant to the manager, summer of 1990

For example, the above listing might look better if it were rearranged slightly:

> Congressional Intern, U.S. Congress
> —Washington, D.C., summer of 1991
>
> Managerial Assistant, Ed's Auto Supply
> —Southold, NY, summer of 1990

If Ed doesn't mind, you might even consider changing the name of his company slightly. Use his *last* name, for instance. This is considered a legitimate ruse de guerre, as is describing a secretarial job as "administrative assistant."

Employers expect you to put the best face possible on your work experience, but they also expect you to be truthful. If this seems like kind of a fine line to you, consider it this way: anything on your resume is a legitimate topic of conversation during an interview, as we mentioned earlier, and most interviewers have excellent bullshit detectors. Before you print out the final draft of your resume, have a friend grill you on each and every item. If anything reduces you to red-faced stammering, it might be better to get rid of it.

Helpful hints from a process server

Irving Botwinick runs a business called *Serving by Irving* which specializes in serving subpoenas to people who don't want to be served. Irving is an expert at getting in to see people. Some of the techniques he and his employees have used:

Say you are delivering a singing telegram

Tell them they have just won the Publisher's Clearing House Sweepstakes

Disguise yourself as a messenger delivering a bouquet

Come up the fire escape

Dress up as a nun

Irving cautions that some of these techniques might not be applicable for the serious job hunter.

Underneath each item you should include a short description of your accomplishments and duties in that position. It has become customary, if not mandatory, for job seekers to use the active voice to describe their exploits. Thus, underneath "Congressional Intern, U.S. Congress" it would not be considered meaningful to write, "general filing and messengering duties" even if that is exactly what you did. Instead, according to the arbiters of resume writing, you must use action verbs: "organized and maintained information retrieval network. Acted as go-between for congressional staff members."

We are, of course, being mildly sarcastic here. Everyone knows that a congressional intern (or for that matter *any* intern) spends 90 percent of his time fetching coffee. The "active voice" will fool no one. On the other hand, you will be considered a wimp if you don't use it. The real key to these descriptions is to find something about your experiences that was different from what anyone might expect. In other words, it will help if you can suggest how you spent the other 10 percent of your time.

Resumes, as anyone who has had to look at two hundred in one day will tell you, can be deadly dull. Anything off the beaten track, so long as it is not completely frivolous, will make your resume stand out. Underneath "Managerial Assistant, Raddison's Auto Supply" you might write, "Assisted in inventory control. On one occasion, personally changed the tire of Senator Patrick Moynihan." Or "Persuaded Raddison's to carry replacement parts for the Yugo—making us the only supplier of Yugo parts on Long Island." Think back over each of your work experiences for standout moments.

It is equally important to show that you actually accomplished something tangible. If you were in charge of a school event, for example, it pays to talk about the result, and whenever possible, use numbers. Instead of writing "Organized a successful annual homecoming dance" you could get specific: "As the organizer of the annual homecoming dance, I oversaw a $6,000 budget, and personally designed an advertising campaign that resulted in a 20 percent increase in revenues over the previous year."

"If I see the word 'liaison' one more time, I'm going to throw up."

(Anonymous human resources person)

More resume blunders:

It's refreshing to see this kind of job-stability:

"Work history: Performed brain wave tests, 1879-1981."

Move over Big Blue:

"Experience with LBM-compatible computers."

This happens to be one of ours, too:

"Personal Goal: To hand-build a classic cottage from the ground up using my father-in-law."

(Source: Accountemps)

ACTIVITIES

Here's where you list sports and school and community activities. Some of these activities could have been listed under work experience; your decision about where to put which experiences will depend on the job you're applying for. In the case studies that follow you will see how the placement of items on your resume can subtly affect the overall message.

The true object of the activities section is to show that you are a well-rounded, normal human being. No employer wants to hire an automaton who is only good at one thing. Outside activities illustrate an ability to work with other people and (in the case of sports and other pressure-driven activities) the ability to work as a member of a team during moments of crisis. Most important, your outside activities hint to the employer that you actually might be fun to have around.

Don't assume that your well-roundedness will come across when you finally get to the interview. If they decide you're a one-trick pony based on your resume, there may not be an interview.

SKILLS, LANGUAGES, PERSONAL STATEMENTS

If you have interesting or noteworthy skills, you might choose to put them in a section all by themselves rather than include them under education. Fluent Swahili, software programming skills, precision skydiving—any of these would deserve mentioning in a separate "skills" section.

Some people like to include a "personal" statement at the bottom of the page such as:

> *Enjoy fine dining, listening to classical music, and long walks on the beach.*

This statement, aside from sounding like a classified ad from the personals, is so generic that it adds nothing positive to the reader's understanding of you. Who *doesn't* enjoy fine dining, listening to classical music, and long walks on the beach? Here's a better example:

> *Avid cook specializing in Tex-Mex, certified PADI scuba diver.*

Guacamole

About 1 cup

  salt
  1 clove garlic
  1 large ripe avocado, pitted
  1/4 teaspoon chili powder
  1 teaspoon lime juice
  2 teaspoons minced onion

Mash all ingredients together. Serve with chips.

This personal statement indicates a serious interest in two unusual areas, and lays the ground for an interesting conversation during an interview. Unless your personal statement will make your resume stand out from the pile it is in, you are better off leaving it out.

REFERENCES ON REQUEST?

Certainly, it is a waste of postage to include reference letters with your resume. If an employer wants references she will ask for them. Some people like to write "references provided on request" at the bottom of the resume. This is fine, although not necessary; these days it is just assumed that your references will be available on demand. Give some thought to whom you will ask to be a reference. Ideally, you want one favorite professor and one former employer.

Many colleges provide a service to their students by keeping letters of recommendation in a central file. Under this system, you have the option when a professor writes you a recommendation of having it put in this file. Then, whenever you need a recommendation, you ask the school to send it out. Thus, you don't have to bother a professor every time you need a reference. If your school does this, it's a good idea to get that letter of recommendation while the professor's memory of you is still fresh. This will also be helpful down the line in case you decide to go on to graduate school or apply for a fellowship. Of course, this recommendation will be of the "to whom it may concern" variety, but they generally are anyway.

It isn't necessary to ask your former employer to write letters in advance, in part because so few employers actually ask to see them. Simply ask your prospective references if they would mind being on call. If they agree, be sure to send them copies of your resume so they will know what you have said about your experience with them.

You may think it is a big imposition to ask former employers and professors to vouch for you, but this is part of their job, and also part of the cyclical nature of the work world. Each of your references has his *own* references on line for the next time he needs a job. And it is not completely beyond the bounds of possibility

"Wait a minute. Can I tell you about my second job?" **Fred Bernstein** wants to know. "Having the first job really didn't help me get the second, I swear."

OK.

"I wanted to write for People Magazine. I'd sent in a bunch of query letters suggesting ideas for stories, but they kept saying no." Finally Fred wrote them a letter about this guy he had found who started out as a Jesuit priest, then became an Anglican minister and finally ended up as an orthodox rabbi. "That one they liked." When he dropped the story off at their offices, he made sure he had several more ideas to pitch. Later that day, the rock music critic at People refused, "as a matter of principle," to do a story about the Village People. They called Fred.

that someday *you* may hire him to work for you or end up writing *him* a reference.

If this person remembers you even semifondly (and why else would you be asking him for a reference?) He will be pleased to hear from you and want to know how your professional life is going. Calling to ask someone to be a reference for you is an excellent way to keep in contact with a valued member of your network.

A "CAREER OBJECTIVE"?

Some resume books recommend that you write a statement at the top of your resume announcing your "career objective." This is most useful when your educational and work experience do not illustrate a clear direction on their own. A career objective statement can help to pull together somewhat disparate educational and work experiences as well as indicate your interest in the job for which you are actually applying.

However, for most people we think the best place to indicate career objectives and interest in a particular job is in the cover letter.

CONSTRUCTING A RESUME: A CASE STUDY

Let's take the fictionalized case of Janet Williams, a senior who will soon be graduating from Lehigh University in Pennsylvania. We're going to describe her for you and then show you two different ways her resume could be constructed.

Janet is a communications major who wants to work as an editor in publishing, although she hasn't decided yet exactly what kind of company she'd like to work for. Her grades are not outstanding—she has a 3.1 GPA, but she has some interesting work experience. Because the job market is tight, she is willing to be flexible and will consider editorial positions in related fields if necessary.

Janet has two job leads at the moment. One is a position as an editorial assistant at a children's book publisher. The other is a position as a junior editor at a corporate in-house magazine. Janet would like to customize her resume for each of these job possibilities. Here is her resume for the children's book publisher:

JANET WILLIAMS

Present Address:
345 South 5th Street
Bethlehem, PA 18015
(215) 555-3333

Permanent Address:
5132 Swan Avenue
Tampa, FL 33609
(813) 555-4444

EDUCATION

Lehigh University, Bethlehem, PA. B.A. in Communications, May 1995. Senior seminar on the role of children's literature in Victorian society. Dean's list 1994–95.

EXPERIENCE

The Philadelphia Inquirer—Summer intern 1994
Conducted research for variety of articles, fact-checked business charts, assisted in copy editing and proofing.

Brown and White (the college newspaper)—Book reviewer 1993–94. Selected books to be reviewed. Wrote over 20 book reviews, including one on *Freud and Fairy Tales.*

Lehigh Volunteers—Teacher, 1993. Tutored first and second graders in English and reading skills.

Deer Lake Camp—Counselor, summer 1993. Led expeditions of 10 twelve-year-old girls on overnight hikes. Told stories around the campfire.

ACTIVITIES

Alpha Phi Sorority—Elected member of governing council, 1994
Fencing Team—Junior varsity, 1993–95

SKILLS

Fluent Spanish, excellent typing skills, familiar with *XyWrite, WordPerfect,* and *Microsoft Word* software programs.

Explanation: We wanted this resume to appeal very specifically to a children's book publisher. Of course, we can't lie or exaggerate her experiences, but we can certainly highlight the experiences that would most appeal to this particular kind of employer. Note that under education we mentioned Janet's senior seminar since it dealt with children's literature. Under work experience, we led off with her most prestigious internship (for *The Philadelphia Inquirer*), which fortunately fits the chronological format. We made sure to emphasize the copyediting and proofing she did there, since that would surely be of use in an editorial publishing job.

Janet's book reviewing experience shows her strong interest in publishing, and because she reviewed so many books, it is not surprising that she could cite one that is sure to interest this particular employer. Janet's tutoring and camp counseling work illustrate that she has experience with—and a sound understanding of—small children. Note how the campfire storytelling is used to bring in the children's publishing angle yet again. The subliminal message here is: "I understand the minds of your audience." Her activities show her well-roundedness as well as her ability to function as a member of a team.

PUTTING ON A DIFFERENT HAT

How can Janet rework her resume to ensure that it will appeal to a corporate in-house magazine? She can't change anything major: her education and her experiences are what they are. However, as you read the resume on the next page, take note of the subtle differences that gear the resume toward a slightly different market:

JANET WILLIAMS

Present Address:
345 South 5th Street
Bethlehem, PA 18015
(215) 555-3333

Permanent Address:
5132 Swan Avenue
Tampa, FL 33609
(813) 555-4444

EDUCATION

Lehigh University, Bethlehem, PA
B.A. in Communications, May 1995.
GPA in major 3.5, Dean's List 1994–95.
Coursework in economics and calculus.

EXPERIENCE

The Philadelphia Inquirer—Summer intern 1994
Conducted research for variety of articles, fact-checked charts on mutual fund performance, whole-life insurance rates of return, and S & L default rates. Assisted in copyediting, proofing, and layouts.

Brown and White (the college newspaper)
Book reviewer 1993–94. Selected books to be reviewed. Wrote over 20 book reviews.

Alpha Phi Sorority
Elected member of governing council, 1994. Made up annual budget, selected vendors, selected pledges, disciplined infractions of rules.

Lehigh Volunteers—Teacher, 1993
Tutored first and second graders in math and reading skills.

Tampa Tattler (high school newspaper)—Features editor, 1991.
Extensive layout and pagemaking experience.

ACTIVITIES

Fencing Team—Junior varsity, 1993–94
Deer Lake Camp—Counselor, summer 1993

SKILLS

Fluent Spanish, excellent typing skills, familiar with *XyWrite, WordPerfect,* and *Microsoft Word* software programs.

Explanation: When Janet was applying for the children's book job, we didn't have to be concerned about her 3.1 GPA, since publishers are traditionally less interested in grades. However, a business corporation might expect to see her GPA. The rule of thumb is that you shouldn't include your GPA if it is under 3.2, but there are ways to get around that. We recalculated her GPA based only on the courses she took for her major. Her GPA in her major is a much more impressive 3.5.

An in-house corporate newspaper will certainly deal with business-related topics, which is why we decided to mention her coursework in economics and math. We don't want to give this company the idea that she is just an artsy communications major who can't add or subtract. On this new resume, the senior seminar now seems superfluous.

When Janet was writing her resume for the children's book publisher, it made sense to gloss over the number-grinding nature of the research she did for *The Philadelphia Inquirer.* However, in the context of this new job, it would be smart to go into specifics about mutual fund performance and the like because it enhances the impression that Janet has a strong business background.

So does her experience on the sorority committee, which is why we moved it up from the activities section and made it part of her work experience. Overseeing a budget always impresses business types.

You may have missed the one change we made in the "Lehigh Volunteers" section. If you check it over carefully you will notice that we substituted the word *math* for *English.* Again, even in very subtle ways, we want the employer to see that Janet is at home with numbers.

The "Tampa Tattler" high school experience was added because an in-house newspaper is bound to involve layout and pagemaking skills. Janet did have some early rudimentary experience in this area, and it made sense to let the employer know.

We moved the camp counselor experience into the "activities" section along with the fencing team. As always, it's important to show that Janet is well rounded.

CUSTOMIZING YOUR RESUME

You can do the same thing for yourself that we've just done for Janet. The best way to begin is to make up a master list of every single noteworthy thing you have ever done. Divide your accomplishments under the three main headings (education, experience, and activities). Then design a general purpose resume, culling the best of your achievements from your master list. Don't be surprised if this takes you several days—as we said at the beginning, writing a resume can be trying. Show your completed resume to a trusted friend who is good with grammar and spelling. Nothing will disqualify you from a job faster than typos and inconsistencies.

Now, each time you apply for a new job, you can read through your master list to see if any of your other experiences apply specifically to this job. It is then only a matter of a few moments to customize your resume.

THE ELECTRONIC RESUME

Some internet services will now post your resume in a database on the internet. Potential employers can access your resume free of charge; you, on the other hand, must pay. Is this worth it? If you're looking for a high-tech sort of job, then it might be. Recruiters and managers from computer and multimedia companies are said to roam the web looking for likely candidates.

Of course, you can eliminate the middleman by sending your resume straight to the E-mail address of prospective employers. This certainly can't hurt, but don't expect anyone to break down your door responding to an unsolicited resume—no matter what newfangled form you send it in. You're much better off *networking* on the internet, and then sending the resume after you've established a connection. For more on this subject, see chapter 7.

Joanna Skoler's senior thesis at Harvard was about the American modern painter David Hockney. In the course of researching her paper she met some museum types who were impressed enough with her to put her in contact with Hockney himself. "I flew out to L.A. and met with him and it was incredible." When it was time to find a job, Joanna wrote a Great Letter. "I got a hold of a gallery guide to New York, and a guide to museums, and sent a letter to, gosh, 30 or 40 galleries and museums." In the letter, she talked about her senior thesis and her meeting with David Hockney. She got several callbacks, and eventually a job offer in New York. "I decided to spend the summer working at camp—which has been my favorite job I've ever had in my life—but because of that the job ended up falling through."

"I was thinking, I have these two roommates and an apartment in New York. What am I going to do? I let myself be down for an hour, and then updated my resume, sent out another 30 or 40 letters, and moved to New York anyway. For three weeks I went on interviews, and got some offers, and finally accepted an offer from a gallery on 57th Street. I think maybe the timing was better the second time around."

An Important Note

Every time you change your resume, even just a little bit, check the spelling—and read it *very* carefully from beginning to end. After all, this is one of the first examples of your work that your prospective employer is going to see.

But it won't be *the* first. A resume is a great tool to show an employer who takes the time to study it just what you have done so far; however, as an attention grabber, a resume has its limitations.

A Great Letter, on the other hand . . .

Writing a Great Letter

We cannot begin to tell you how important a Great Letter can be. It can change everything. It can make mediocre grades superfluous. It can make indifferent work experience irrelevant. It can get you in to see someone who is impossible to see. The Great Letter is the beginning of everything.

What Makes a Great Letter Great?

Remember what we said all employers want? *Passion.* A Great Letter conveys your passion to work for them. It should also demonstrate your intelligence, with just a touch of humor thrown in for good measure. If you can combine these three elements in a one-page letter, you are halfway in the door already.

Like any cover letter, a Great Letter should be laid out in business format, single spaced, with a line between each paragraph. It should be short and snappy, never contain a typo, and never seem mass produced. You may be sending it to fifty people, but it should read as if *this* letter could only have been written to *this* one prospective employer about *this* one job.

You may not be able to write a Great Letter to every employer. Why? Simply because you won't feel passionate about every job possibility, and *you can't fake passion.* They'll know if you try.

So What Happens When I Can't Write a Great Letter?

You write a good one. A good letter is the next best thing. It conveys all the same things: your interest in the job, a brief summary of your credentials, an understanding of the industry. In fact, you may not even know when you've written a good letter and when you've written a Great Letter. But you'll find out when the phone rings.

We Know What You're Thinking: Talk Is Cheap

Okay, we'll show you a certified Great Letter. Jon Hein is a young screenwriter recently out of college. He decided to write to eighty producers in Hollywood. As everyone knows, it is impossible to get to producers in Hollywood without an agent. Jon was told no one would even read the letter unless it was sent through a lawyer.

So why did *forty* producers get back to Jon? Here's the letter in its entirety, and we do mean entirety. You have to be feeling pretty cocky to write a three-page Great Letter. Obviously, Jon got away with it, but we recommend that you keep yours to one page.

Dear xxxxxxxx,

A million to one.

The *Hollywood Reporter. Premiere* magazine. My skeptical parents. They all agree on my chances of bringing a comedy to television.

While attending the University of Michigan in the mid-eighties, I directed and produced *Comedy Company*, a university-sponsored comedy troupe, for three years. *Comedy Company*'s average audience went from 150 to 2,250 students during my tenure.

People at Michigan liked the stuff, so that knocks my odds down to 911,000 to 1.

Upon graduating from the University of Michigan, I attended a seminar where Lawrence Kasdan was speaking. He glanced my way.

Every little bit helps, and we're down to 816,000. Michigan has extensive alumni.

Based on the success of *Comedy Company*, I was able to book shows at Northwestern, Notre Dame, Michigan State, and other area colleges. All of the shows sold out, and the troupe was asked back for the next semester.

The Big Ten obviously liked what it saw, so that drops me to 654,000. Notre Dame's an independent, so make it 650,000 even.

But away from scholastics and on to the hard knocks of the real world. With Michigan no longer footing the bill, I decided to create and produce *Just Kidding*, a nationally touring sketch comedy troupe based on *Comedy Company*'s success.

Great idea, but where are the shows? I'm stuck at 650,000.

On its own, *Just Kidding* booked 100 shows at campuses across the country in just one year. From Washington, D.C., to Pocatello, Idaho, people paid good money to see *Just Kidding*, and coast to coast it left them laughing and wanting more.

A proven national audience drops me to 325,000 to 1.

While on the road, *JK* performed with the likes of Mario Joyner, Robert Klein, and unknown stand-up comic Tim Allen.

You never know who will become a star. 250,000.

Just Kidding was approached by lots of agents. We chose one.

Who doesn't have an agent? We're steady at 250,000.

After one year, I realized that our hustling did more than this agent would ever do for the troupe.

100,000 to 1.

As *Just Kidding* continued to grow, I heard L.A. calling. So I sent a pitch letter, and Gary H. Miller, executive producer of *A Different World*, Jay Kogen, producer of *The Simpsons*, and Sara Brock, of a new series, *Home Improvement*, requested spec scripts.

Real television industry experience drops me to 25,000 to 1. I knew that a connection would pay off someday.

This past summer, *Just Kidding* won first prize in the Entertainment Division of the Hometown USA Video Festival sponsored by the National Federation of Local Cable Programmers.

An Emmy? An Ace? No. But an award-winning thirty-minute TV special shot on a $173.14 budget takes my numbers down to 10,000 to 1.

Saturday Night Live. In Living Color. Kids in the Hall. Sketch comedy is on the rise, and *Just Kidding* has comparable experience, a national audience of 18 to 24-year-olds, hundreds of proven sketches, and no one on the disabled list. Besides, we're funnier.

This brings me to 1,000 to 1. Not bad, considering where I started, but a brief phone conversation with you would certainly help my numbers.

I'll be calling you soon. Thanks for your time and consideration.

Sincerely,

Jon Hein

P.S. The original cast of *Just Kidding* is performing in Ann Arbor, Michigan (our alma mater), on Saturday, October 3 in the 1,400-seat Power Center. If you'd like to check us out in person, I'd love to fly you there. Please give me a call at (xxx) xxx-xxxx.

So, you've written your cover letter and your resume. How should you send them once they're done?

OVERNIGHT MAIL

Have you ever received an Express Mail package? The deliverer rushes up to your door and rings the bell insistently. He hands you the package in its brightly colored envelope that practically screams "Urgent!" and you have to sign for it. Everything about this experience is designed to make you feel that you have just received an extremely important communication.

It seems only fitting that your cover letter and resume should arrive with this same kind of fanfare. Even if your prospective employer is not there to see it delivered, he will probably get to see the envelope it arrived in. So, until *everyone* starts using Express Mail delivery, it may make sense to spring for the extra postage.

SHOULD A RESUME EVER BE FAXED?

If an employer says, "Why don't you fax me your resume?" then of course, you should fax it pronto. The employer is practically promising fast action. However, in general, faxing a resume is not such a good idea. For one thing, you have no control over what the resume will look like by the time it comes out the other end of the employer's fax machine (the quality of these machines varies wildly). Better to send it by express or regular mail.

However that is not to say that the facsimile machine has no use at all in the job search. Faxes lend themselves to short, snappy communications; they are perfect for quick follow-ups.

We know of one job hunter who, after not hearing from a prospective employer to whom he'd already sent his resume, faxed the guy a note that read,

I'll give you $1,000 to read my resume.

He then faxed ten hundred dollar bills (well, it may just have been one hundred dollar bill ten different times).

A few minutes later, the employer faxed back "the change"—several coins. Apparently he only charges $999 and change to read resumes. For what it's worth, even though the employer had a sense of humor, the job hunter did not get a job. The moral: faxed notes can keep you in your employer's mind but beware of cute ideas.

Professions With the Worst Male/Female Ratios		
	male	female
Mining and extraction	98.9	1.1
Firefighting	98.6	1.4
Construction	98.0	2.0
Dentists	93.5	6.5
Engineers	93.3	6.7
Architects	88.7	11.3
Physicians	82.8	17.2
Lawyers and judges	81.8	18.2
Natural scientists	79.2	20.8
Advertising & PR marketing	76.2	23.8
Math and computer scientists	68.8	35.2
College and university professors	64.8	35.2
Financial managers	64.3	35.7

(U.S. Bureau of Labor Statistics)

USING THE TELEPHONE

There are going to be times when you want to speak to your prospective employer in person, and other times when you would rather not, but the one person you don't ever want to speak to is the employer's secretary. Part of a secretary's job is to get rid of people who call about jobs. If you *do* get the secretary, be cordial and try to find out his name in case you have to speak to him again. Of course, it is much better if you can bypass the secretary completely.

The best times to get through to the boss directly are between 8:30 and 9:00 in the morning and between 5:00 and 7:00 in the evening, when no one else is there. Keep in mind the reason the *boss* is there is to try to get some work done before people arrive and start asking questions. Thus when you reach him, he is probably not going to be thrilled to hear from you.

Ah, but what if you called at midnight instead? Well, it's true your prospective employer probably won't be there, but if her company is one of the ever increasing number that have installed voice mail systems, then you have just been given a wonderful gift: a forum to state your case.

VOICE MAIL

Voice mail is an aural Great Letter. Imagine this scenario: you call an intimidating, very-hard-to-reach prospective employer who has not responded to the three messages you've left with his secretary, only this time, instead of getting the secretary you hear the employer himself saying,

"Hi, I'm away from my desk right now. Please leave a message of any length."

Gather your thoughts quickly. Or better yet, hang up and call back when you know just what you want to say. This is your chance to talk to him directly. Again, you are trying to communicate passion, intelligence, and a sense of humor. Even though the machine will presumably keep recording for hours, be succinct and to the point. Suggest that you will call back in a few days. If he liked your message, he may well take your call.

Of course, the best way to get an employer to take your call is if someone else has already told him about you.

Connections and Networking

The word connections conjures up images for some people of oak-paneled university clubs where young men wearing rep ties get hired over cigars by captains of finance who prepped at Exeter with their fathers. We aren't saying this kind of thing doesn't happen, but this is actually a very narrow definition of "connections."

Everyone has connections, whether they realize it or not. A connection, according to our definition, is simply a person who thinks well of you. Are you trying to say that no one thinks well of you? What about your mother?

Okay, so your mother is not the chairman of General Motors, but she may well know someone who knows someone else who is a vice president of General Motors. Sometimes the link can be incredibly tenuous—"My best friend's uncle knows this guy who goes out with the hairdresser of Madonna's personal manager." Obviously, in a chain this stretched out, you cannot expect a warm personal recommendation from Madonna's personal manager, but with persistence and a good attitude you may eventually be able to get an introduction to the person you really want to see.

So as we say, everyone has connections; the problem is that no one really wants to use their connections. Partly, it's that desire to do it all yourself. You don't want to owe anyone, and you want to make it on your own merits. Partly it's because new graduates feel so incredibly awkward about approaching an old family friend—or a previous employer or an uncle or the father of a friend—in the first place.

"WHAT DO I SAY?"

How do you even approach a "connection" about a job? It's always hard to toot your own horn, even more so when the person is important or imposing. Feeling awkward about the situation can make you botch it up—either by giving the impression that you simply assume the person will hire you without question, or by being so tentative that she (a) doesn't even understand what you are asking for or (b) gets the impression you really don't want to work for her anyway.

HOW CONNECTIONS WORK

You will feel much better about using connections once you understand what the process is really about. First of all, a connection, except in very rare extreme circumstances, can do no more than get you in the front door. The rest is up to you. The woman in charge of the analyst program at one of the major investment banks puts it this way: "Say Joe Smith is the chairman of this who knows the chairman of that, and the next thing you know, his kid has an interview. Well that's fine as far as it goes, but after that the kid really is on his own." Thus, any feelings you have that you are getting something you don't "deserve" should be thrown out the window. In most cases, all you're getting is an introduction.

Second—and this is the thing people have trouble believing, even though it's gospel true—you are not imposing on them. Employers are always on the lookout for fresh talent. It's part of their job. If they discover someone who eventually gets hired and does well for the company, it is a feather in their cap.

Third, people enjoy being asked for advice. It's flattering and fun for employers to have someone sit at their feet while they dispense wisdom. Many employers don't have a regular forum in which to discuss their work philosophy, and they'll welcome the chance to tell you all about it. And if you hit it off, they'll often be willing to go way out of their way to help. Never underestimate an employer's desire to mold, to shape, and to mentor.

"WHAT IF WE DON'T HIT IT OFF?"

As long as you both go into the meeting with the agenda set up in advance, there's honor on both sides, no matter what the outcome of the meeting. Exactly what is the purpose of this meeting? You want to find out about this person's profession and the company he works for; he wants to get a look at you. That's it. If things proceed any further it's because both parties decide they want it to happen. You might be turned off by his work environment; he might not like your resume. But neither of you is going to be so impolite as to say so out loud, and in either case no lasting harm will have been done. He will not feel that you have rejected his entire worth as a human being if you send him a nice thank-you note and never call him again. You should not feel that he has rejected your entire worth as a human being if he gives you some helpful information and sends you on your way.

You are not just looking for a job, you're looking for a fit. You want your skills and interests to intersect with a company's needs and opportunities. One of the ways you'll know you've found a fit is when you like the people you meet at the company; another is when they like you.

NETWORKING

Let's look ahead for a moment. Let's assume it's five years from now. You took all our advice, found a good job, worked hard, and now you're ready to jump to a higher paying job with increased responsibilities at another company. So how do you proceed? That's easy. You put out the word to your professional colleagues—the people in your industry who have worked with you and know just how good you are. Some of them have moved on to other companies themselves, so they can recommend you for jobs with their new employers. Some of

William Manger took the summer off after he graduated from Trinity College, and then came to New York to find a job in the art world. "I tried applying for some of the gallery jobs advertised in the classifieds, but I wasn't even getting a chance to interview." He also applied to the New York auction houses, but couldn't get past the human resources people. Bill started networking. "It turned out that a friend of mine knew the owners of an art gallery and he put me in contact with them. I interviewed, but they were unsure about whether they really needed someone. So I persevered and called and called and called, and finally they asked me to come in again, and they offered me the job two days later. I started out at the bottom of the totem pole, of course, as an assistant."

Jenny Horst majored in theater at Wesleyan. After she graduated, she came to New York to find a job in the theater. A friend of a friend suggested she call the theatrical producer Jed Feuer. He invited her to come to his apartment for an interview (this sort of thing happens in the theater). When she rang his buzzer, he came out to the front door of the building to let her in, and the door to his apartment slammed shut. "I'm standing in the hallway with this producer in his socks, and he's locked out of his apartment." Jenny took out a credit card and burgled his front door. Did she get the job? Are you kidding?

them are still at your present company, but they know other people who work elsewhere. Some you may have met through your professional association or through projects that involved you with outside companies.

In very short order, you've got a whole network of people out there looking for your next job. Why? Because they know you're excellent, and they either want to bring you in to work with them at their company, or they want to make themselves look good by recommending you to another company. And also, naturally, because they expect you to do the same for them.

Once you get this first real job, you will begin to build your own network—people in your field who believe in you and think well of you based on your performance in that field. Every day that you come in to work and do a great job and relate well to the people around you, you are building your own personal network. It's a great feeling, and believe us, it will make job hunting much less traumatic in the future.

"OKAY FINE, IN FIVE YEARS I'LL BE SITTING PRETTY. WHAT DO I DO NOW?"

Now, you begin by using other people's networks.

Toward the end of an interview with a connection, you should ask if he can think of anyone else you should see in his field. Chances are he will be willing to give you the name of someone in another division or at a different company. Ask if you may use his name. If you've been polite and haven't made him uncomfortable by acting like you expect him to do any more than give you advice, he will probably let you use his name, even if he doesn't think you are exactly right for him.

In this way, you expand your own network of contacts. When you meet with the person he recommended, you will again be there to find out information about his profession and his company. He will, again, be checking out the new talent. And again, you might hit it off, in which case you've found a valuable ally, or then again you might not, but either way you'll be sure to ask him if he can think of anyone else you should see in his field. And he will probably give you another name to add to your growing network.

COMBINING CONNECTIONS AND NETWORKING

The average job hunt takes several months, and includes a couple of false starts and heart-stopping near misses. Thus even if you have a fantastic lead on what you think might be the perfect job, you should still pursue all the other options we've already discussed and will be discussing in the coming chapters—including your college career placement service, help-wanted ads, and employment agencies—preferably all at the same time. The more effort you put in, the faster you will find the job you're looking for.

However, one of the most important parts of the job hunt is the careful combination of connections and networking. The two are closely related; remember, we defined a connection as someone who thinks well of you. Well, networking is merely the process of expanding the number of people who think well of you.

HOW TO BEGIN

First, do your homework—find out everything you can about your prospective profession. When you go in to talk to someone, you don't want to waste her time with questions you could have found the answers to in last week's Wall Street Journal. By the time you are ready to talk, you should be as much of an expert in your prospective field as an outsider can be. We described a bunch of different sources of information on professions in chapter 2. However, now you want to go even further, and get information on the specific companies of the people you're going to go see. If possible, get their annual reports (sometimes available at college career centers, the public library, or through the public relations department of the company itself). Also look to see if they have web sites on the internet. While both annual reports and web pages are often so slickly written that it's difficult to make heads or tails of them, you can at least get an idea of their different holdings, and read the party line to see how they say they did last year. You should also scan recent newspapers and trade journals for any new developments.

Liz Reilly majored in economics at Boston College, and knew that she was interesting in the marketing side of advertising. "In my junior year I did an internship at Seagrams in the U.K. for an entire term. It worked out really well, so they put me in touch with their New York division, and I worked in their events marketing department over the summer before my senior year."

In her senior year she "did some interviewing on campus, but there was nothing I was really excited by. I was going to be a volunteer for the Peace Corps, but then my brother's best friend, who was much older—in his mid *thirties*—offered to help me. His first job had been at the advertising firm D.B.D. Needham, and then he went off and started his own firm. I flew down to New York to meet him, and he gave me some contacts. I went on a bunch of informational interviews, including one with a man in human resources at D.B.D. Needham." It turned out that Seagrams (where she had done her internships) was one of D.B.D. Needham's bigger clients, so of course Liz's resume and references were that much more impressive. "They flew me back down and I went for 'rounds' (a full day of interviewing) and they gave me the job. I actually started out with a client-based position at Mobil Oil."

Now It's Time To Talk To Connections

Take a deep breath, and pick up the phone. It's time to talk to the people who think well of you. These might include (but are not limited to) previous employers, your parents, friends' parents, parents' friends, friends, college alumni, and members of your church or social organization. If you're lucky, one or two of these people may actually work in your target industry. If not, they may be able to hook you up with someone else who does.

How you get in touch with connections depends on your relationship to them. If they are people you customarily talk to in person or on the telephone, then that is the way you should approach them now. For example, it would be appropriate and normal to call up a friend who was a year ahead of you in college. On the other hand, it might be better to write a letter to a more august alumnus whom you have only met once or twice.

Keeping Track

The name of each person you contact should go into your Rolodex (What? You don't have a Rolodex?) correctly spelled, with his job title, company, address, and any personal information you have about him. (It may seem plastic and phony on your part, but people really do like it when you ask how their kids are—particularly if they have kids.) As one contact leads you to another, you'll keep adding new names. This Rolodex is the beginning of your network.

It's a good idea to write down when and how you contacted someone and when you said you'd get back to him. Many people find the toughest part of job hunting is the follow-up phone call. They don't mind writing letters. They don't mind going on interviews, but making the phone call, "to see if you got my letter," drives them crazy. To avoid procrastinating, it helps to set aside a specific time during the day to devote to this (as we said in chapter 5, between 8:30 and 9:00 A.M. and 5:00 and 7:00 P.M. are your best chances of getting straight through to the boss). If you are having trouble making phone calls, you might consider forming a job hunter's support group with a friend or two. In addition, pursuing

When **Mary Wessely** finished her design degree at the University of Texas, one of her friends had a father who ran an architectural design firm. Her girlfriend arranged an interview. "It was pretty easy to get that job because what they ostensibly needed me to do was a lot of gofer stuff—pulling resource materials from the libraries, getting together bids for projects. Then I started doing blueprints for them on a freelance basis, and after a while it developed into a full-time job as a design assistant."

Gilbert Warren wanted to get a job in advertising sales. When he graduated from Denison University, he knew just how to proceed: "I relied on family friends," he says, somewhat mysteriously. Gilbert was brought in to interview for a sales assistant position at *Sports Illustrated*. "I did some research beforehand, and the interview went pretty well. I guess they liked what I knew about the company and the skills that I said I was hoping to learn there."

several leads at once helps to put rejection in perspective, and multiplies your chances of success.

If connections and networking aren't getting you in to the one person you most want to see, try writing a Great Letter (as described in chapter 5) directly to that person. Unless he is inundated with mail, he is likely to get back to you. But when you finally do get through to the person you want to meet, just what are you asking that person to do for you?

THE NOT-QUITE-INFORMATIONAL INTERVIEW

In chapter 2, we said an "informational interview" was a great way for someone who was curious about a particular profession to learn about it by talking to someone in that profession.

Let's assume that you are no longer just curious. You have now definitely decided this field is for you. However, you just can't go in to see a connection (no matter how close) and say:

> *"Hi. Remember when I was a baby and used to sit on your knee and act adorable? It's payback time. I want a job."*

The etiquette of these situations says that it is up to the connection to decide what kind of help he wants to give you. And if this is not a personal connection but someone you're meeting for the first time through networking, this kind of behavior will get you put out on the street.

Therefore, whether this is a family friend or a friend of a friend of a friend, the best approach is still to ask for an informational interview. You have come for advice. However, during this informational interview, you are going to be asking for very different information. Instead of asking what it's like to be in marketing, you will now be asking about which area of marketing he thinks is expanding the fastest and might be able to use a bright, hardworking, eager-to-learn person such as yourself.

Your questions will be much more specific, and will impart to your interviewer the depth of your knowledge about his field. It should be clear to him that you are now committed to his field, that you have done your homework, and that you would love to be offered a job.

Linda Harkrader majored in finance at Lehigh University. When she graduated, she knew she wanted to be involved in the market. She called an old friend of the family who was the head of a small money-management firm. The woman agreed to hire Linda on a temporary basis. "She said, come work for me; you can see all the different aspects of what we do, and then you can figure out where you want to go from there." What was the interview like? "She had known me for years, so I didn't have to interview."

However, you are not begging. The closest you might come to the subject of your own employment is to ask if he knows of any openings that might be coming up. The impression you want to leave behind is that of a bright, energetic young graduate who has not only taken the trouble to learn quite a bit about the field but is also easy to get along with, tactful, and confident.

The main thing to avoid is changing the rules in the middle of the interview. Employers hate being put on the spot; if you said you wanted information, don't turn the interview into a plea for a job. Of course, if the employer brings up the subject, what can you do? If this happens, sit back and enjoy the ride.

However, most of the time, an interview like this is meant to end inconclusively. No one said there was a job that needed filling; this was not a job interview (which we will cover in chapter 10). You were there to ask lots of wonderful questions and try to look as smart as possible. The next day, you can send a thank-you note, and ask that he keep you in mind for future openings. Your note, like your demeanor during the interview, should be appropriate to the industry you want to enter—not too outrageous for banking, not too staid for the music industry.

And always remember to ask if he knows of anyone else you could talk to.

STILL FEELING UNEASY ABOUT USING CONNECTIONS?

Let's discuss your worst fears: they just want to hire you so they can laugh at you; they want a favor from your parents; they feel sorry for you; they want to sleep with you. Well, these are all possibilities. But there are lots of other reasons someone might want to help you, and many of them are pretty altruistic: maybe you remind them of themselves when they were your age, or they think you can help them, or they think you can make them look good for recommending you, or maybe someone once helped them get started and they want to do the same for you. Maybe they actually even think you're right for the job.

The Wired Way to Get Hired

THE WIRED WAY TO GET HIRED

Of course, if you *really* hate talking to people in person or on the telephone, there is one other way to make connections: the internet.

The explosion in career-search opportunities on the Net has been called "nothing less than a revolution" by *Fortune Magazine*. Today, it's theoretically possible to conduct your entire job search—from researching potential professions, to downloading resume prototypes, to career counseling, to networking, to the actual interview—without ever going off-line.

Naturally, anything that's getting this much hype has to be taken with a grain of salt. The internet (a network of linked computers from all over the world) is not some panacea that will have you employed before lunch. As one of its main proponents, James Gonyea, author of *The On-line Job Search Companion* says, "The only thing that's changed is the *medium* of communication. The communication itself is what you make of it."

Still, the new job search opportunities on the internet are pretty astounding. In order to participate in all this you'll need any old computer, a reasonably fast modem (14.4 or higher) to attach to your phone line, and some kind of monthly internet service that provides access to the World Wide Web, the easier-to-use part of the internet.

Once you're up and running, the net can help you in virtually every area of the job search.

JUST LOOKING

If you're still in the exploration stage, you'll find profiles of every sort of career in the career centers of most of the commercial on-line services such as America OnLine, Prodigy, and Compuserve.

Once you've narrowed your focus to a particular field, you can search the Web for interesting sites pertaining to that field using a web directory; Yahoo (http://www.yahoo.com) is a particularly good directory. Just type in the subject you're looking for and start exploring. Many web sites have hypertext links to other sites. For example, an aspiring astronomer might visit the Kennedy Space Center web site, then click on a highlighted word, which would send him to a university web site where he might select another highlighted word that leads him to the personal home page of a NASA astronomer.

For in-depth Company profiles, you can visit Hoovers Handbook of Companies (http://www.globeandmail.ca/GIS/content.html); or see if the company you've targeted is one of the 10,000 (and counting) corporations that have created their *own* web pages. According to college career counselors, an increasingly frequent question during job interviews these days is, "Have you seen our web site?"

Not only do you *not* want to look blank when they ask that question, you want to be able to say, "Yes! I liked it much better than that of [insert competitor's name here] because [insert three good reasons]." Besides, this is the easiest way there is to get specific information about a company. You might as well take advantage of it.

Just remember, the information a company chooses to present on the World Wide Web will tend to be as rosy as its full-color glossy brochures. For more hard-hitting commentary, you might want to look up the company's recent stock performance (available from any

How many people are on the internet? It all depends	
According to the Nielsen study	
The internet	24 million
Commercial on-line Services	40 million
America Online	10.5 million
According to the Vanderbilt study	
The internet	10 million
Commercial on-line Services	10 million
America Online	4 million

(Source: New York Times, 1995)

of the brokerage services found on the commercial internet services), or scan the web sites of The New York Times (http://www.nytimes.com) or The Wall Street Journal (http://update.wsj.com) for business news articles from the past year.

INFORMATIONAL INTERVIEWS

If you want to find out more about a particular field, you can sit in on forum discussions or read news group correspondences related to that field. (Lists of forums and news groups can be found all over the internet.)

For example, someone interested in journalism might join a news group called "alt.journalism.objective" where she might find working journalists debating the ethics of paying a news source.

Of course, you'll be tempted to jump into these discussions right away, but hold back until you're confident that A) you understand internet etiquette and B) you have something relevant to say. These discussions can be incredibly interesting, or incredibly mindless (there's no way to predict in advance). But either way, it's a chance to hear professionals talking about the issues they deal with every day.

MAKING CONNECTIONS

It's also a chance to get their internet addresses so you can send them an E-mail later on. It may seem strange to write to a complete stranger, but if you do it correctly, the odds of getting a response to an E-mail are much higher than if you wrote a snail mail letter to someone about whom you know nothing.

Consider: you've just read a message posted by this person or listened in on a live chat in which he took part. So you know his position on some issue, an this gives you something to talk about in your E-mail.

However the same rules we've discussed regarding phone messages and cover letters still apply here. Be concise. Find a way to demonstrate your intelligence and your enthusiasm for the field. And, unless you believe you've already made a real connection with the person, don't ask directly for a job.

Average job tenure in the United States

1984: 12.5 YEARS
1994: 7.0 YEARS

(Source: Money Magazine, 1994)

The Perils of E-Mail

One of the great advantages of E-mail is also its great disadvantage: its informality. People who never write letters love E-mail because it seems so off-the-cuff and unintimidating. Unfortunately, this informality can be the downfall of a job-seeker. It's so easy to toss off an E-mail that you can be lulled into less than perfect grammar, ill-considered remarks, and perhaps worst of all, claims to expertise you don't really possess. "Chinese? Of *course* I speak Chinese." A good way to nip this in the bud is to compose all your job-related E-mail *before* you log on. This way you'll have time to reflect, edit, and spell check.

If people write back to you, remember they may be receiving several hundred messages a day. When you respond, don't assume they'll remember exactly what you were talking about last time. Try to summarize your previous exchange briefly, even if you're responding almost immediately. You might also take the advice of an AT&T interactive television executive who said that he gets too many messages a day to even bother reading an E-mail from a stranger—unless it has a catchy heading.

On-line Chat

If a prospective employer responds to your E-mail, you may want to suggest meeting on-line in a private chat room for the equivalent of an informational interview. Have your questions ready—in fact, you might consider pre-typing them in a word processing program, along with some intelligent sound bites (spell checked) so you'll be able to copy and paste them into the conversation.

This will ensure that at least part of your side of the conversation will appear exactly the way you intend it: intelligent, informed, concise.

Career Counseling

If you need career counseling along the way, and can't or won't use the counselors at your college, it's available on the internet. If you have only a couple of questions, you might get them answered for free during one of the informative chat sessions held by the AOL Career

Center counselors. For more in-depth counseling, you'll have to pay for a private session, available from practically all the services we've already mentioned.

ON-LINE CLASSIFIEDS

Once you've figured out what field you want to be in and learned everything you can about its culture, it's time to start looking for a job. One disadvantage of traditional classified ads has always been the lag time between when an employer calls in the listing and when you actually read the ad in the newspaper. Internet classifieds have the potential to be much more up-to-date. They also bring you access to a wider pool of listings.

For example, consider The On-line Career Center (http://www.occ.com). This web site has 262 corporate members each of whom pays $3900 to join, plus $2400 a year to list their job offerings on the internet. The service is completely free to job hunters.

Or try On-line Classifieds (http://www.careerpath.com) which contains the daily combined help-wanted sections of six of the nation's largest newspapers, including *The New York Times* and *The Los Angeles Times*. This service is also free to job hunters.

ELECTRONIC RESUMES

Another way to go is to pay to have your resume listed in a database that is free to the *employers*. For example, The America Online Career Center charges a modest fee to post your electronic resume for an entire year. The companies that run these databases say employers scan these resumes closely every week.

Some independent career counselors suggest that if you are extremely computer literate, it might pay to write two entirely different electronic resumes. The first, designed to get you in the virtual door, should look like a normal resume. The second, to be sent once you've established some kind of a connection, might be a multimedia presentation complete with graphics, audio, even video. Obviously this would be more likely to help if you're hoping to land a job in multimedia software than if you're looking for a position as a research chemist.

23.6 cents to go

In 1979, women earned 62.5 cents for every dollar men earned.

Today, women earn 76.4 cents for every dollar men earn.

The Club

On the other hand, employers are increasingly looking for computer literate employees. It makes sense that certain types of jobs would be advertised *only* over the internet: for example, jobs for web page designers and CD-ROM programmers. But even if you're looking for a job as a librarian or a forest ranger, being on the net is a good way to show prospective employers that you're computer literate.

To some degree, the internet is like an exclusive club. Not everyone belongs, and so far, this exclusivity has been helpful for job seekers. Many club members have been willing to extend a helping hand to other members. Of course, the membership requirements keep becoming less stringent all the time—at this point, it's estimated that 20 million people are on the net. As more and more people get wired, the clubby atmosphere of like-minded techno-nerds will inevitably be weakened and job seekers may find that their electronic resumes will have no more cachet than their paper resumes.

It's Exploding

But that's not going to happen anytime soon. The explosion of interest will bring huge numbers of new employers to the net just as it brings huge numbers of job seekers. The only thing we can say with certainty is that the internet world is changing so quickly that by the time you read this, there will be many more career-oriented services available—so don't stop with the web sites we've described. Pick a directory, and crawl that web.

Employment Agencies, Career Counselors, and Head Hunters

The word you hear over and over again at employment agencies is *flexibility.* Says Kathy Klein in charge of recent graduates at Career Blazers, a national employment agency, "If you're a communications major and insist that you will work only for a financial magazine, then you are closing yourself off to many opportunities, and we may not be able to help you. However, if you're willing to be *flexible,* then we might be able to get you a full-time position on, say, the staff of an in-house magazine at an investment bank. Real opportunities exist today, but you have to look off the beaten trail."

As employment agencies see it, the beaten trail is for the lucky graduates who got recruited while still in college. "We can be very helpful for people who fall right below that line," says Randy Schaefer of Rand Associates. "Not that we don't sometimes get very high-level assignments as well." The assumption seems to be that top-tier candidates have already been snatched up by employers. Now, the scramble is on for the remaining jobs. "There are thousands of resumes flying around out there," says Kathy Klein. "These kids need an advocate."

How Employment Agencies Work

Critics of employment agencies charge that an advocate is precisely what young graduates are not getting. Most employment agencies are paid by the employers rather than by the individuals who come in looking for work. You might think this would be an ideal arrangement, since unemployed people don't have the money to pay a fee anyway. But what it means is that employment agencies essentially work for the employer rather than the employees they place at companies. It would not be surprising if the agencies were more interested in pleasing their client (the employer who pays the bill) than the young graduates who fill the slots. Obviously, a business that wants to stay in business has to pay attention to its paying customers.

However, the agencies point out that it isn't in their interest to try to fit square pegs into round holes. "It would not make any logical sense to press someone into a situation that's not going to be good for them. They'll just leave," says Schaefer. "At Rand, we offer a guarantee period of thirty days. If a situation doesn't work out because either the employee or the employer is unhappy, then we don't get paid."

Still, you are unlikely to get the same kind of caring attention at an employment service that you can sometimes find at your college career office. For one thing, employment agencies are very busy. "Like the employers themselves, *we* are inundated right now with college grads," says Klein. "So if applicants aren't focused or if they are completely unrealistic about their expectations, we aren't going to help them." In addition, employment agencies want you to take one of the jobs they have on their books now. If you try to hold out for something better—well, you're not being *flexible*.

What Can You Expect from an Employment Agency?

When you arrive, you will be interviewed by a counselor, and perhaps given a typing test. These days, skills such as typing and word processing are particularly vital, according to the employment agencies. "They have to be willing to barter skills for learning experience," explains

Klein. "They have to be willing to type, do computer work, while they learn." If a statement like this makes you think that the kind of jobs you can find through employment agencies are heavy on grunt work, you are probably right.

As we've already said, *all* entry level jobs have their share of unglamorous details, which you are expected to grin and bear. According to Schaefer, in the present economy, "jobs are very entry level. They may appear to be glorified secretarial positions, but the clients have assured us that these positions are promotable. We're looking for someone who's bright. It is the person who is promotable, not necessarily the job."

She has a point. In the final analysis, any entry-level job is just a launching platform for your talents. If you are curious (or *passionate*, as they say in the soap opera trade), a hard worker, and good with people, then your abilities will probably be recognized even if you are stuck in the mail room. A first job is not necessarily the crucial first step that some people try to make it out to be.

However, it's a lot harder to be curious (or passionate) if you take a job in a field that doesn't interest you. This is an ever present danger with employment agencies, where there are usually paying jobs lying around unfilled. With student loan payments looming, it is easy to get a little *too* flexible and end up working in a job that holds no interest for you.

WHAT KIND OF CAREER COUNSELING IS AVAILABLE AT EMPLOYMENT AGENCIES?

Obviously, this varies quite a bit. Agencies tend to specialize in one field or another. If you go to an agency that only supplies computer programmers to banking firms, then you should not expect to be sat down for a heart-to-heart talk about your career options. Nor will you get much sympathy if you confide to them that what you really want to do is direct. As far as a specialist employment agency is concerned, you indicated a career choice just by showing up on their doorstep. Some of the nonspecializing agencies do a good job of finding out what you are good at and what you want.

When **Jenny Robbins** finished Sarah Lawrence, she was pretty sure she wanted to be a teacher, not a lawyer, but she decided she owed it to herself to give law school a try. "I figured I would start with a summer term (the school allowed you to do that) and if I didn't like it, I could still find a teaching job for the fall." Just as she had predicted, she hated law school. With only a few weeks to go before the beginning of the fall term, she applied to Carrey-Sander, a well-known teacher placement service. They found her a job teaching in a small, all-girl boarding school located in Amish country in Pennsylvania.

"The job included living with the girls, and I think my mental age regressed several years in as many months. I stuck it out, though, and learned a lot—but it was a hard year." She spent a lot more time and thought finding her next job, and is much happier now.

What kind of counseling can you expect at a nonspecializing agency? Says Schaefer, "We sit down with you and try to help you become more realistic, try to get a concept of what makes you happy, of what excites you, and then we tell you what's available, at what salary ranges."

Don't Sell Yourself Short

While learning to be realistic may be a good idea for the majority of new graduates who walk in the door dreaming of glory and a key to the executive washroom, without any idea of what it is they really want to do, it may not make sense for you. Sometimes words like *realistic* and *flexible* carry with them the aroma of defeat. It seems clear that part of the employment agency message is that we all need to lower our expectations a little. "They are probably not going to find the job they dreamed of—at least not to begin with," says Klein.

If employment agencies have a bad rap, it is perhaps because of their reduced expectations. When you read some of the horror-show descriptions of bad employment agencies in other job guides, you might get the impression that the people who work there are sadistic monsters who stay awake nights thinking up ways to get honest, hardworking college graduates to give up their dreams. But in fact, like anyone, the people who work in employment agencies want to feel good about what they do. They would like to find you a job that makes you happy. When employment agencies talk about realism and flexibility, it is partly because they want you to take their jobs, but it is also partly because their advice has to be tailored to the majority of the people who come through their offices—and the majority of these people don't know what they want.

Knowing What You Want

Imagine an employment agency waiting room filled with job seekers. In some ways all these people look the same—they're all wearing suits and fidgeting—and most of them, when you ask them what kind of career they want, are going to mumble that they're not really sure. Maybe something in business, preferably in the high thirties.

"The most important thing on a resume is quality internships, or substantial work during the summer. People come in to us, and they can type 50 words per minute, but they have no idea how to write a business letter."

—Kline

But one or two of the people in that waiting room are going to be emanating an aura that an employment agency person can spot in a New York minute. It is the aura of someone who knows what he wants. As we've said before, *you* are not just anybody. If you have discovered a field that fascinates you and have taken the trouble to learn all about that field, you are going to shine like a beacon in that office.

How to Get an Employment Agency to Give You Its All

To get real value from an employment agency, you have to walk in the door knowing exactly what you want, and not be afraid to stick to it. Employment agency personnel are just like real employers; they are impressed by someone who is confident, who has done her homework, and who has a plan. If you present yourself this way, they are much more likely to try to find you your dream job.

Thus it is important to show the employment agency the same professional picture you would present to an employer. Arrive on time, well dressed, with a notebook, a vision, and a great attitude. "If they tell me, 'I really want to work. I'm flexible, I'm interested,' that is going to impress me," says Schaefer.

The agencies are also impressed if you are willing to "make a commitment" to them, which generally means signing a contract. An employment agency contract should specify who pays the fee if you are hired (usually the employer) and under what circumstances a fee is owed (usually only if the *agency* finds you a job). Though some agencies will push you to sign an exclusive contract, it is not necessary and they should not insist. We recommend that if you want to go the employment agency route, you follow accepted practice and sign on with several agencies at the same time. However, read all contracts carefully before you sign.

The Temporary Route

It is much easier to stick to your guns and hold out for the job you are really interested in if you are eating regularly. Many employment agencies have an office

Salaries for engineers under 30

WOMEN: $39,132
MEN: $37,693

(Source: Working Woman, 1994)

temp division, and allow people seeking full-time work to take temporary assignments as secretaries or administrative assistants while they're looking.

There are several possible advantages to this. First, by doing well at your temporary assignment, you will show the employment agency that you are on the ball and deserve a shot at their best full-time listings. Second, you earn enough money to keep up your dignity (and your car payments). And third, you may impress the company you are temping for so much that they will offer you a full-time job.

The third alternative is an advantage only when you actually want to work for them. If the job offer doesn't fit in with your aspirations, don't let their enthusiasm and money seduce you from your true path.

What if you truly have no aspirations? You've thought about it long and hard, you've talked it over with everyone, and you still don't know what you want to do with your life. Again, office temping might be the answer. Like internships, temporary positions let you try out different fields for a few weeks or months at a time. Unfortunately, you probably won't get to do any meaningful work while you're temping, but you will be able to get a sense of the culture of the profession, as well as get to know some of the people who work there. These short-term assignments can help you look for the field of your dreams.

How to Find an Employment Agency

The best way to choose an employment agency is through referrals. If a friend you trust has used a particular agency and recommends it highly, that is a good indication that you will find people there who are on your wavelength. If your friend has dealt with a specific counselor at the agency, ask if that person is still there and available for consultation. When you go in to visit, see if you get a good feeling from the place. Are the receptionists friendly? Does the counselor you talk to seem to be really listening? What kind of support do they offer in terms of interview practice and resume consultation? Do they seem knowledgeable about your field? If they don't, they probably won't have many jobs in your specialty.

CAREER COUNSELORS

It is only when you start looking into hiring a private career counselor that you really start to appreciate your college career center. For $50 to $200 per session, a career counselor will provide most of the services your college career center gave you for free.

Counseling, vocational testing, resume doctoring, practice interviewing, job listings—these are all valuable things. In fact, at $200 an hour, they are obviously much more valuable than you ever suspected. Traditionally, career counselors have existed for people who are changing jobs or changing careers, rather than for new graduates. However, this is changing slowly, and there are several reasons why you might choose to hire a career counselor.

For example, some college career centers are much better than others. If yours is inadequate or understaffed, if you have a personality conflict with your adviser, or if you have been out of college for several years, then it might be worth your while to talk to a private career counselor.

There are a few outstanding professionals out there—some of them probably better than the staff at the average college career center. On the other hand, there are also a lot of just plain bad amateurs, and unfortunately it is often hard to tell the difference on first meeting. Certainly you should not equate quality with a large fee. "This is not one of those situations where you necessarily get what you pay for," says Nella Barkley, president of the prestigious Crystal Center located in New York.

WHAT TO LOOK FOR

The first rule of thumb is to try to get a recommendation from someone who had a positive experience with a counselor, or ask for a referral from a college counselor you trust. If you are in any doubt about a private counselor, contact the Better Business Bureau in your area. Unfortunately, they will only be able to tell you if there have been complaints about a particular counselor; for some reason, the BBB doesn't keep track of good service.

Second, you should never sign on with a private counselor before you have met him, and decided that you have a good rapport—if he doesn't understand your

Drawing by Tom Toles
©The Buffalo News

need to be, for example, a park ranger, he will not be able to see the forest for the trees.

Third, stay away from companies that try to sign you up for some hideously expensive package deal, and want all the money up front. Most reputable companies will let you pay as you go. It is also probably wise to avoid a company that refuses to discuss its fees over the telephone.

How long should the counseling process take? "This is not a time for quick fixes," says Barkley. "People should be willing to spend at least as much time planning their careers as they spend, say, planning their next vacation."

If this sounds *expensive,* it can be. However, there are a number of ways to make it less so.

CAREER WORKSHOPS

A cheaper alternative to one-on-one counseling is to take a career counseling workshop. It might seem useless to have to take time out to listen to other people's career conundrums, but in fact it is sometimes easier to see solutions to other people's dilemmas than to your own, and you may be able to see something about yourself by looking at someone else. A group situation also creates a feeling of solidarity and shared misery, which can be very beneficial.

CAREER COUNSELING VIA MODEM

All the major commercial on-line services offer some sort of career counseling over the internet. You pay by credit card and get to chat with a counselor via modem. The fee is generally a lot less than it would be to meet with a counselor in person, and if you are located some distance away from a good counselor, this might be the way to go. Of course, you can't cry on a virtual counselor's shoulder.

A COUNSELOR IS NOT A SURROGATE

It is tempting to think that by hiring a professional, you can sit back and relax while he or she does the work. Unfortunately, it really doesn't work that way. Coun-

Remember **Alisa Gilhooley**, who was laid off in a Holiday Inn (along with her entire division) three weeks after she moved from Chicago to New York to start her fist job working at a corporate magazine? With two weeks' severance pay in her pocket, and a year's lease on an apartment, she decided she was going to find another publishing job in New York. "I'd heard a lot of bad things about head hunters as far as recent college grads are concerned, but I went to see this head hunter and she found me a job that was perfect for me. She'd done a lot of work for this particular publishing company and seemed to understand that my strengths were just what this company was looking for. At the interview, I clicked with my potential boss right away." Of course, she still hasn't set foot in a Holiday Inn.

selors see their role as helping job seekers define their goals. Many counselors do not even keep lists of current job openings. As far as they are concerned, it would be a disservice to deprive a job seeker of the growth opportunity that a really tough job search provides. Yeah, and cod-liver oil is good for you, too.

Of course, no matter how much money you pay, a counselor cannot get the job for you. Most of the work will still be on your shoulders—as it should be. Nobody else cares as much about your career as you do. A good counselor can help smooth the way, but you are still the one who will be making the phone calls, sending the resumes, networking, and interviewing.

HEAD HUNTERS

Executive recruitment firms are the crème de la crème of employment agencies. Typically, they specialize in corporate high-level posts. There are two kinds of recruiting firms. The first is a retainer firm. Retainer firms are generally hired by a corporation to find, as one corporate executive puts it, "someone you need that you don't have, either because you've just perceived a need, or because someone's just gone under a bus." Retainer firms are paid regardless of whether their work results in a hire. Unfortunately, it will be several years before you are going to be in a position to take advantage of their services. They are looking for experienced talent, mostly in the $100,000 a year and up salary range.

You may be saying to yourself, "Well that's fine. I don't mind starting at the top." Don't even bother sending a resume. The head hunters we spoke to were blunt: "We're looking for very specific talent," a top retainer executive recruiter told us, on condition that he remain anonymous, "and college grads just don't meet that category." He adds, "You've got to understand that executive search firms often work by targeting companies, and trying to entice talent away from these firms." In other words, even if you have years of experience and lots of talent, it is still much easier to be recruited by a retainer head hunter when you are already employed.

The second type of recruiting firm is called a contingency firm. Contingency firms are paid only when their work results in a hire, and are perhaps a couple

When **Liza Charlesworth** graduated from SUNY Binghamton, she moved to the East Village in New York City, and waitressed for a while. "I guess I just wasn't ready to start a career," she says. "My friends had all prepared—you know, they went to their college career centers and stuff, but I had this huge block about doing my resume. I just couldn't. I finally got my sister to do it for me." When she started looking for a job in publishing (her career of choice) she realized that there was one small stumbling block— she kept flunking their typing tests. "I finally went to an employment agency that specialized in publishing. They said, 'Look, why don't you come to work for us here. You can polish up your typing, and when you're ready, we'll find you a job.'" Why does Liza think the employment agency offered to hire her? "You can't act like you're entitled to the job. I think I communicated that I was willing to go in there and roll up my sleeves and work hard. The people at the agency were pretty lame—they talked about their fur coats all the time—but I learned a lot about office skills, and after all, it *was* a personnel agency, so of course I learned more about how to find a job." Liza learned so well that inside of a year (and without any help from the agency) she had started her career in publishing.

of notches down in prestige. According to David Lord, who puts out the *Directory of Executive Recruiters,* contingency recruiters can sometimes be talked into handling a newly graduated college student. "They might be willing to market a candidate who has something, who they think is attractive. We suggest candidates send a resume, a brief cover letter, and don't telephone. The odds are one in a thousand, but it's worth a try, especially if you have a degree in accounting or computer science or other technical skills."

If you don't like odds of one in a thousand, you might want to try the classified help wanted ads, where the odds are somewhat better—perhaps as good as one in four.

Classified Ads

The experts all agree. Answering classified ads is in-effective. According to the 1972 census report that everyone always quotes—the report based on a survey of ten million job seekers—answering help-wanted ads in local newspapers had an effectiveness rate of 23.9 percent, and answering ads in nonlocal newspapers had an effectiveness rate of only 10 percent.

There are two reasons we disagree with all the experts. First, an effectiveness rate of 23.9 percent translates into over *one million* people every year who find jobs through the classifieds (.239 times the 4.59 million people who according to the survey actually attempted to use the classifieds). Second, that percentage would be even higher if people knew how to use the classified ads more efficiently. Granted, networking and your college place-ment center are your best bets for gainful employment, but you should never disdain the help-wanted section.

WHERE TO LOOK

Classified ads are normally found in three separate kinds of publications: national, local, and professional trade—and these days you can also find them on the internet, as we've already described in chapter 7. We'll speak about the pros and cons of each; however, the real trick is to find out just where the ads you're looking for are placed, and then to concentrate on them. Over time, it has become a matter of custom for particular businesses to place their ads in particular corners of the classified sections of particular publications. This is not to say that there will never be any ads for, say, futures traders in *The Miami Herald,* but a future futures trader will have a lot more luck looking in the New York and Chicago papers—where the markets are located. By the same token, a teacher who looked only in the classified section of *The New York Times* would be missing a large number of education ads that for arcane reasons appear each week in the "Week in Review" section.

This is the kind of information that you will pick up along the way as you go about immersing yourself in your prospective profession. In informational interviews with people who are only a few years ahead of you, it helps to ask them how they found their jobs. They will often be willing to share the job-hunting strategies that have been effective for them.

Job guides recommend that you read the alphabetized want ads cover to cover since job descriptions can start with practically any letter. For the first couple times you look in a particular periodical, this is good advice. However, you will soon get a sense of where the jobs you're interested in are located.

As you scan the classifieds, you are not necessarily interested in finding only the entry-level jobs. Often, when a slightly more senior job is advertised, it means that there will be a shake-up in that department. Perhaps in the game of musical chairs that follows they are going to need an entry-level person as well.

INTERNET CLASSIFIEDS

For truly up-to-date job listings, it's hard to beat the internet. We've already listed some classified resources in our chapter on the on-line job search. If you have access to On-line Classifieds (http://www.careerpath.com), which contains the daily combined help-wanted sections of six of the nation's largest newspapers, then you may not need to get the paper version of the national classifieds listed below.

THE NATIONAL CLASSIFIEDS

There are now two nationwide weekly compilations of ads. *National Ad Search* is a weekly roundup of classified help-wanted ads from seventy-two different newspapers from across the country. To order, call 1-800-992-2832. *The National Business Employment Weekly* is put out by *The Wall Street Journal*. It lists all the help-wanted ads run in the four regional editions of the *Journal* during that week.

The drawback to using these compilations is that your cover letter and resume are often going to arrive several days behind those of the people who saw the ad in its original incarnation, or on the internet. The response to classified ads varies tremendously. Some are said to generate as many as three thousand responses. These responses usually pour in within the first few days after the ad has run. Thus if you see an ad in one of the compilations, it may already have been seen (and been responded to) by many people in the local market where it first ran. If the employer was in a hurry to fill the slot, the job may already be gone. On the other hand, the employer may be in no hurry to go through that huge pile of resumes, in which case, yours will be near the top of the pile when it's finally gotten around to.

LOCAL CLASSIFIEDS

Many career counselors believe that when you are answering want ads, the more local the newspaper, the better. It costs less to advertise in smaller newspapers, which means that the ads they run tend to be from smaller companies who don't yet have lots of money to waste on help-wanted ads. You might think this is a drawback, but in fact, small companies offer many advantages to a first-time job seeker. For one thing, they tend to have a much more streamlined hiring process; they're generally too small to have a human resources department, which means that you will probably be interviewed by the person you would be working for. Small companies also typically have more room to grow, and greater opportunities for advancement.

In the minus column is the possibility that they will go out of business. However, small companies don't have a monopoly on this kind of behavior. And even if it were to go broke, a small company that lets its entry-level employees take on real responsibility will provide infinitely more valuable experience and ultimately look better on your resume.

TRADE CLASSIFIEDS

It might take some digging, but getting current trade publications is always worthwhile—if only for the background you will pick up about the culture of your chosen profession. Some of these trade papers have classified sections as well. Since trade publications are geared to professionals, there will be fewer entry-level positions advertised. However, you will get a good sense of which companies are hiring or firing, and as we've already said, an opening for a more advanced job implies another opening farther down on the food chain.

To find trade publications and industry newsletters look them up in any one of the following:

- *Gale Directory of Publications and Broadcast Media,* Gale Research, Detroit, MI; published annually.

- *Hudson's Subscription Newsletter Directory,* Margaret Leonard, editor, Rhinebeck, NY, 1990.

- *Standard Periodical Directory,* Oxbridge Communications, Inc., New York, NY, published annually.

- To find professional organizations
  (which may have their own job listings
  on a bulletin board somewhere), look
  for *The Encyclopedia of Associations,*
  Gale Research Inc., Detroit, MI.

All these books can generally be found in a good public library.

WHAT PERCENTAGE OF HELP-WANTED ADS ARE PLACED BY EMPLOYMENT AGENCIES?

Employment agencies place a large number of help-wanted ads in major newspapers, but it is difficult to say exactly how many. According to laws on the books in many states, employment agency ads are supposed to be clearly labeled, but you will find that this is not always the case. In 1990, The consumer affairs branch of the city of New York investigated fifty employment agencies who it said were running ads that did not properly disclose that they had been placed by employment agencies. A representative from the New York Consumer Affairs Department says that, three years later, things are "much better." There are fewer deceptive ads (at least in New York), but the agency ads remain. Are they ever worth answering?

Critics say that some of these ads are for jobs that do not exist. Employment agencies might run fake ads in order to attract new talent to the agency, or for the purposes of what is called "bait and switch." An applicant could be told, "Sorry that position has been filled, but we just happen to have *another* position you might be interested in." The agencies say that in their fast-paced efforts they just sometimes fill the jobs faster than the newspapers can print them. The truth is probably somewhere in the middle.

If you decide to answer an agency ad, keep your expectations under control. Send your resume and a generic cover letter. Most likely, you will be invited in for an interview at the agency. If they like you, regardless of whether you get the advertised job, they will probably call you from time to time with other possibilities. If you liked them, then you can call them back.

Andrea Paykin was in no particular hurry to find a job after college. Her parents understood completely. " 'Take your time,' they told me." Several months later, they told her to leave and not to come back until she'd found a job. "It was very unlike them," Andrea says, loyally. She went through the help-wanted ads and saw one that seemed interesting, working as an editorial assistant at Daniel Weiss Associates—a publisher that puts out romance novels. The advertisement said, "resumes only—no calls."

Andrea figured that going to see them in person wasn't really a call, so she turned up and talked her way in to see the guy who was going to make the hire. "He had a huge pile of resumes on his desk. He looked at the resumes, looked at me, and said, 'I can't deal with all these resumes,' and hired me."

Two Things to Look Out for: 800 Numbers and Bogus Training Programs

An increasing number of help-wanted ads ask you to call an 800 number. This can sometimes be legitimate, but be careful. In some cases, you will find that your phone call will be answered by a recording asking you to call a 900 number for additional information. If you make that second call, all you will receive will be a huge charge on your next phone bill. Another scam you may run across is a help-wanted ad that turns out to be a training program you would have to pay money to join. Reputable newspapers want to know about deceptive advertising, so take a vindictive moment to call the newspaper in which you found the scam ad, and get someone in trouble.

We don't mean to give you the wrong impression. The vast majority of help-wanted ads are just what they appear to be.

Responding to a Help-Wanted Ad

To the extent you have time, you will want to customize your resume (as we showed you in chapter 5) for each want ad to which you respond. The employer is likely to be swamped with replies, and one of the ways he will cut down on the number of people he has to see is to throw away all the resumes that don't fit *all* the requirements set forth in the ad.

If the ad asks for "some knowl acctng" you will want to stick into the education section of your resume a reference to the accounting course you took in your sophomore year, or play up the bookkeeping you did during your summer job. If an advertising ad reads "pharm exp pref'd" you can rack your brains for any pharmaceutical experience you may have, and hope that there wasn't a typo and they didn't really want someone who knows about crop rotation.

John Lavine wanted to get into radio when he graduated from Boston University. "My *intention* was to buy a van and head across the country auditioning for radio stations until I found a job. I bought the van, but it was a lemon and broke down with a regularity that both astonished and pleased the repair shops of Boston." After spending all his money replacing virtually every component in the engine, he saw a classified ad for a DJ at the Naked i Cabaret. "I stood outside looking at this place with the flashing red lights, and thought, 'you really can't do this,' but I did. I auditioned, and got the job, and it paid the bills until I found a job in radio."

Your Cover Letter

In most cases, the cover letter you write can't be too specific since you won't know very much about the company you're applying to, or the position being offered. In some cases, you won't even know the company's name. Your cover letter should, however, indicate your knowledge of the field.

Many career counselors recommend that a cover letter in response to a classified ad be very short and to the point. Volunteering any more information than asked for can get you typed out without an interview. The sole purpose of this letter is to show you have the very qualifications they are looking for and to intrigue them enough to want to see you in person. As always, they will have no interest in seeing anyone who can't spell, so be sure to proofread your cover letter.

The Armchair Job Seeker

Answering classified ads obviously has its merits, but it is only one part of the job-hunting process, and you do not want to neglect the others. It is easy to spend the morning scanning the want ads and sending out resumes. Then, as Felicia Brings of Brings Results, a career counseling consulting company in New York, puts it, "You and Phil and Oprah and Montel spend the day together waiting for the phone to ring."

It is scarier but much more effective to get out into the trenches. You can put it off for a while, but you will eventually have to meet someone in person in order to get a job. Remember, one day the phone actually *will* ring, and you will be invited to an interview.

The Job Interview

In the preceding chapters we described at some length the informational interview, basically defined as an interview conducted when there is no specific job on the table. An informational interview can run the gamut from a beginning exploration ("I'm thinking I might want to go into finance. Could you tell me what it's like?") to a more advanced networking interview ("I've become fascinated by the junk bond market. I know that you were one of the pioneers in this field, and I was wondering if, once you get out of prison . . .").

This chapter is going to be about the other kind of interview—the kind given when there is actually a job on the table. There are lots of similarities between informational interviewing and job interviewing: the biggest and most important similarity is that a job interview is still a two-sided process.

FINDING A FIT

You haven't done all this thinking and research and informational interviewing in order to take just any old job. You are looking to match your skills and interests to the company's needs and opportunities. They will be asking you questions. You will be asking them questions.

If the answers to all these questions are mutually satisfactory, then things may proceed to the next level. Now that you've discovered what *you* want, you need to find a company that will let you do whatever that is.

WHAT "THEY" WANT

You already know what employers want: they want youth and they want passion. The first you've already got; the second you're probably well on your way toward acquiring if you've been taking our advice in the previous chapters.

Now it's time to go in and show *them* that you have what they want. The youth part will be self-evident. It's the passion part that requires practice—not because you don't have it but because not everyone finds it easy to articulate something that is fairly personal and may sound a bit dorky when you say it out loud.

"HI, MY NAME IS . . . "

Let's talk about the interview from hell. You're waiting in the anteroom feeling pretty confident, when across the room a flawlessly turned out fellow interviewee in an outfit that must have cost $2,000 takes out his Montblanc pen and makes a confident little note on a legal pad, and suddenly you simply lose the will to live. All the information you have carefully researched, all your enthusiasm, all thought of triumph . . . no, let's be frank—all thought—vanishes from your head. Your mind is a blank as the secretary calls out your name and you march like a prisoner toward the gallows. At the doorway stands your interviewer wearing a suit and a somewhat inscrutable-looking Mona Lisa smile, holding out a hand to be shaken. You grasp the hand firmly, trying not to throw up, and look the person in the eye, as you've been taught to do.

He peers at you uncertainly and says, "And you must be . . ."

There is a long silence while you try to remember your name. "Come on!" you rage at yourself. You knew it a minute ago. This is not that tough a question. You finally remember, and blurt it out like it's the winning answer on *Jeopardy!* The interviewer looks at you like you are mold growing on a piece of bread and says, "So. Tell me about yourself." The cubicle isn't completely soundproof, and in the gathering silence you can hear gales of laughter coming from the adjoining room as that future captain of industry with the fancy pen holds his interviewer enthralled.

COMMUNICATING PASSION

It can't get any worse than that, right? And even if you had the worst interview of *your* life, it won't be as bad as some of the ones that human resources people talk about among themselves. Probably the most comforting thing is that all those people—the ones who cried during the interview, or farted, or didn't wear socks, or tried to slap the interviewer five—all of them probably eventually found jobs, once they'd learned to tone down their act and communicate their real interest.

Knowing what *you* want makes you intensely attractive to employers. As Nella Barkley puts it, "Nothing sells like genuine interest." However, if you can't communicate your interest during the interview, you aren't going to have a chance to show it to them later on.

How do you communicate your passion?

PREPARE

One of the best ways to show your interest is by exhibiting a working knowledge of the field you would like to enter. This means having done your homework, including all the things we've talked about in previous chapters: scanning the newspapers for articles pertaining to your field, reading trade journals, going on informational interviews, understanding the culture of your prospective profession.

You should also have some sense not just of where your profession has been, but where it might be going. What innovations lie ahead? What problems remain to be faced? None of this means that you have to become a walking encyclopedia. For example, no one is going to ask you what the industry gross revenues were last year.

Top Ten Most-Often Asked Questions by Interviewers

1. Tell me about yourself.
2. What do you see yourself doing five years from now?
3. What is the accomplishment of which you are most proud?
4. What do you know about this company?
5. Why do you want to work here?
6. What is your greatest weakness?
7. Describe a difficult situation in your life, and how you handled it.
8. What did you think of your last job?
9. Why aren't your grades higher?
10. Read any good books lately?

Researching an Individual Company

Your preparation for an interview with a particular company doesn't have to be all-encompassing either. An understanding of the field is much more important. However, you *do* need to know exactly what the company does, what its current problems are (only as background—whatever you do, don't bring them up during the interview. As a conversation stopper, "I hear the IRS is breathing down your neck," is way up near the top of the list), their goals, and whether they've been in the news lately.

If you can, it also helps to find out about the person who will be interviewing you for the job. What is her exact title? How long has she been with the firm, and what are her accomplishments? The best way to get this type of information is not from books like *Who's Who in America,* but from other people in the field. For one thing, the information will probably be more up-to-date and more down-to-earth, and for another, a call to someone else in your network to tell them that you are in serious consideration for a job is never a bad idea anyway.

You might think that if you were passionately interested in a field and had done your homework, that that would come across in any interview. Well, it will. But like almost anything that you want to do well, interviewing takes practice.

Soundbites

Like a politician running for office, you have to learn to get your soundbites in no matter what question you are being asked. Let's visit a master of the form for a quick tutorial. Let's imagine Ted Koppel wants to ask Bill Clinton about the deficit. Bill Clinton wants to talk instead about the need for a new trade agreement.

Appearance Checklist

- ✔ hair washed and combed
- ✔ No bad smells emanating from anywhere on your body
- ✔ No overpowering good smells emanating from anywhere on your body
- ✔ Suit or nice dress freshly ironed
- ✔ Shoes shined
- ✔ matching socks (men only)
- ✔ matching earrings (women only)
- ✔ a minimum of makeup (men and women)

Koppel: *Mr. President, it has been suggested that you have not done enough in your first one hundred days to bring down the deficit.*

Clinton: *Well, that's a very interesting suggestion, but before we can even*

*address that question I think we have to
go to the root of the problem: unfair
balance of trade agreements signed by
two Republican presidents that have
stifled American competition up to now.*

What if Koppel had asked instead about Socks, the
White House cat?

Koppel: *Mr. President, has your cat, Socks,
shown any signs of anxiety about having
to succeed Millie, who was, after all, a
bestselling author?*

Clinton: *Socks is doing just fine, but Ted, I want
to make sure that Socks is still doing fine
in a couple of years, when restrictive
trade agreements will have crippled our
home cat food industry unless we do
something now.*

It really didn't matter what Koppel asked; Clinton
was going to find a way to segue into what he wanted
to talk about—his agenda.

YOUR AGENDA

In *your* interview, you are going to have an agenda as
well. You will want to develop and practice soundbites
to reinforce each item on your resume, and soundbites
to answer the questions most often asked by interviewers.

If an interviewer does not ask about what you think
is an important point, you will want to bring it up.
Sometimes interviewers get rattled and forget to ask
about a subject they really meant to cover. Later on,
when they are filling out the printed form that many
companies provide for interviewers, they will have to
either leave that section blank or make something up
based on their hazy memory of you.

Other times, interviewers will try to go easy on you
and not bring up a subject out of some misguided sense
of tact. For example, if you dropped out of school for
a year, and the interviewer fails to bring it up, it is in
your best interest to mention it yourself and put as positive

a spin on it as possible. Later on, when the interviewer is deciding whether to hire you or call you back, an unresolved issue like this can start making him wonder. If you haven't talked about it this episode will be just a question mark to him, with sinister possibilities. Why did she drop out? Why didn't she want to talk about it? Hmm.

SPIN DOCTORING

To avoid this kind of speculation, you particularly want to practice your responses to questions about the troublesome issues from your life. Everyone has something from his past that he is less than thrilled about. However, with some practice you can turn these liabilities into bonuses. For example, if you dropped out of school temporarily, you might say something like this:

> *I had lost my focus. I wasn't sure anymore why I was studying to be a computer software designer. Maybe after doing so much mental work for so long, I needed to do something physical. I got a job working on a construction project, and it really helped me regain my focus. Naturally, I couldn't help noticing that the computer program the on-site architect was using had several bugs, and I actually managed to fix them. Somehow, after that, I knew that I was on the right track.*

WHY DO THEY INSIST ON TALKING ABOUT THE HARD STUFF?

In the same way that a playwright looks for moments of crisis in his characters' lives to help define them to the audience, an interviewer looks for your moments of crisis to define your character for her. She's looking for the times when you had to make a decision or rise above adversity or live up to a commitment. The one C– on your transcript. The term you transferred to another college. The time you came in second in the debate.

This may seem unfair, but the real world has its share of crises, and your interviewer wants to know if you'll be able to handle that. Thus, if you present your life as an episode of *The Brady Bunch,* your interviewer will have no idea how you will perform in moments of trial. The trick is to anticipate the tough questions and be prepared.

Sometimes, the interviewer will let you pick the moment of trial, by asking, "What was your most frustrating work experience?" or "What is your worst fault?" Either question is an open invitation to reveal a carefully rehearsed period of crisis *that you were able to overcome*. Sometimes, the interviewer will pick the moment: "I notice from your resume that you didn't have a job or internship last summer. Why?" By practicing at home, you have already come up with as good a spin as you can to explain what happened last summer. Just remember, interviewers like angst—as long as you learned from it, and came away stronger.

"I'm afraid that's classified, sir."

COMMUNICATING PASSION: A PRACTICAL EXAMPLE

Remember Janet Williams, the made-up student from Lehigh whose resume we wrote in chapter 5? Let's say that she has gotten an interview at the children's book publisher she was interested in. Janet wants to practice her responses to a few likely questions. She gets together with a friend who is also in the process of interviewing and they take turns asking each other tough questions. One of the most important responses to rehearse is your answer to the question, "Why do you want to work for us?" This is a tailor-made opportunity for you to communicate your passion for the profession. In fact, this point is so important that if the interview is nearing its end and you haven't been asked this question yet, you should just follow the example of your president and segue right into it. Here's an example of what Janet might say:

> *"I've wanted to work in publishing since I was about twelve years old. My parents didn't let us watch TV after dinner. We would all sit around the living room reading, and I guess the habit has kind of stuck. I've also always had a soft spot for children's books. I've about worn out my copy of* The Little Prince, *and I*

chose to focus on a related topic for my senior thesis. My work experience showed me that I like working with copy, and I think I have a talent for layout.

"Basically, I think you're the perfect company for me, and I just hope you feel the same way about me."

BUILDING CONFIDENCE

No matter how heartfelt, Janet's answer to this question would not be as effective if she hadn't thought it out beforehand, and actually practiced saying it out loud several times. It takes practice to become confident in your interviewing skills. If you still have access to your college career office, the mock interview is one of their more valuable resources. Many schools now offer classes in which your responses to questions are videotaped for later dissection.

Nothing will cure you of an annoying verbal tick (such as prefacing every sentence with a "You know" or an "Uhh") faster than counting up how many times you used it in the first minute of a videotaped interview. The same is true of bad posture, cracking your knuckles, bobbing your head from side to side—you name it. Seeing is believing, and you will be astounded that your family and friends have let you walk around for twenty years without telling you what a dork you look like.

While it is great to get to see yourself on videotape a couple times, once you have cured yourself of your most obvious bad habits, it is probably just as valuable to get together with a serious friend and interview each other using a tape recorder. Even though it will seem ridiculous, practice answering the same questions several times until you feel comfortable with them. Of course, you don't want your responses to sound rehearsed or routine. Practice delivering your soundbites as if you had never thought of them until just this minute.

Can They Speak in Complete Sentences?

"I don't have any particular questions that I ask. The point is not so much the question, or even their answer to the question, as how they answer it. Can they speak in complete sentences? If they can, then they can probably write in complete sentences as well."

(Lawyer)

"I Hate to Brag"

People often find it hard to toot their own horn. When asked about a part-time job they will say, "It was just a secretarial job."

Felicia Brings, who counsels job seekers says, "When I'm dealing with someone like this, I'll say, 'Fine, it was just a secretarial job. But when you started the job, what was the filing system like?' Invariably, it was a mess. So I ask, 'What did you do about it?' And invariably, it turns out she had completely reorganized the filing system. People don't know what their own assets are."

For every item on your resume, you should practice talking about what you actually accomplished in that position. Don't be afraid to brag. Your interviewing partner will let you know if you're going over the edge.

The Interview

The initial job interview will take place either in a small cubicle on campus (if it is part of the recruitment program) or in the employer's office. It can last from twenty-five minutes (if it's a recruitment interview) up to several hours. Be sure to get there early. Eat something ahead of time. Go to the bathroom and check your ensemble in the mirror right before you go in.

The Three Types of Interviewers

When you meet on campus, you will probably be interviewed by a volunteer from the company who has only been out of school for a few years herself. When you meet at the employer's office, if the company is a large one, you will probably be interviewed by someone from the human resources department (formerly known as "personnel"). If the company is a small one, you may be interviewed by the person you'd actually be working for if you got hired.

There are advantages to all three. You might be less intimidated by a young almost-contemporary who went to your school. She will probably be young and enthusiastic, and once she has established that there is nothing wrong with you, she will tend to be on your side. On the other hand, a human resources person may be a much

---

Have They Sweat Yet?

"Summer work experience in our field counts an enormous amount. Lots of people are smart, but you have to have had the experience of sweat running down your brow, because a team project isn't finished and it isn't even your fault, but you're a part of this group and it has to get done tonight and it has to be perfect."

(Investment banker)

better interviewer. After all, these people interview for a living. A good interviewer knows how to cover all the bases, knows how to compensate for the unreality of the interviewing situation, and has a lot more practice in remembering who you are the next day.

An initial interview with the boss you'd actually be working for is incredibly useful because you both get to see if you get along. A boss is also more likely to take a chance on someone he gets a good feeling about—even if one aspect of the person's qualifications is weak. By contrast, human resources types, at least by reputation, are more likely to screen out someone who doesn't fit *all* the minimum requirements.

HUMAN RESOURCES

Some counselors maintain that you should avoid human resources departments like the plague. According to these counselors, human resources people are totally run by their fears that they will fail to screen out someone who will embarrass them later. Thus their primary function has become to say *no*.

There are three reasons this advice isn't useful. First, in some organizations, at least at the entry level, there is no other way to get hired except through human resources. Second, there are good and bad human resources people just as there are good and bad bosses. The odds that you will find a good human resources person (who understands the pitfalls of just picking homogenized, bland, politically correct people) are probably no worse than the odds that you will find a good boss. And third, no matter how great the boss is, she probably only has one job to give away. A good human resources person can put you up for a variety of jobs within the organization.

ASK NOT WHAT THEY CAN DO FOR YOU (AT LEAST NOT OUT LOUD)

It is easy to get the impression during an interview that the subject of the interview, the *star* (so to speak) of the interview is, well, you. After all, you're the one in the hot seat. You're the one whose life is being dissected. Don't be too flattered. The real subject of the interview is the company. The company is what the interviewer ultimately thinks is important. This isn't about your ambition, or what the company can do for you. As far as the interviewer is concerned, it is about what you can do for the company.

Of course, *you* will be very concerned about what opportunities and skills the company has to offer you, but if you're smart, you'll keep that to yourself. It's not that it isn't proper to be interested in advancement and money—in fact, that's pretty much a given. What is not a given is your ability to put the interests of your company ahead of your own from time to time; to make personal sacrifices for the good of an important project. The interviewer will be extremely interested in these things if you can find a way to communicate them.

ASKING YOUR OWN QUESTIONS

All this is not to say that the interview is not a two-way street, or that you can't ask questions. You need to know to what extent this job will give you the opportunity to learn about and participate in your field of choice. What could be more proper than asking questions about that? Some sample questions:

> *Can you define what my responsibilities might be?*

> *What level of client contact should I expect?*

> *What are the characteristics of a person who has been successful in this job?*

Even better are specific questions you have about the company that have come out of your research, particularly if they flow out of the conversation you've been having.

THE SECOND INTERVIEW

The second interview will be more of the same, except that it will take longer, you will meet a lot more people, and there may be a meal. Try to keep all the names straight, don't order a drink at lunch, and don't spill anything if you can help it. When you're asked the same questions over again, as you will be, try to be consistent,

Easygoing individuals

"I look for people who are easy to get along with, but that's not to say they should be pushovers who will say 'yes, I'll do anything' in a robotic way."

(Magazine editor)

but don't repeat yourself word for word. If you've made it this far, they already like you. Relax, but carefully.

MONEY

All the experts agree. Try to put off all discussions of money until it is clear that they really want you. As a new graduate, you will not have a huge amount of bargaining power anyway, but you have a right to bring up another offer if you have one, to see if they want to match it. We will discuss this in greater detail in chapter 15.

HOW DO INTERVIEWERS THINK?

We decided to turn the tables on the woman in charge of interviewing analysts at one of the top investment banks in New York. Her advice will be particularly valuable for people applying to investment banks, but we think anyone looking for a job will find it interesting to see how a professional human resources person thinks. Here's how the interview went:

So, Tell Us About Yourself.

"The bulk of what I do is interview entry-level analysts. It's a highly competitive process. First, students send resumes through their colleges. The schools they went to are very important for one thing because we can only interview at so many schools, and we only have so many slots. If someone doesn't go to one of these schools it's going to be harder for that person to get in to see us. Not impossible. We have a procedure to examine every resume

---

that's mailed to us. It's harder to attract our attention if you come from a school that's not as competitive. An A is not an A at every single university."

Do You Think Grades Are a Good Indicator of Abilities?

"Grades signify a desire to achieve. Admittedly, there are people who focus only on grades, but we look for people for whom doing the best is important and that's reflected in their GPA, especially if they do other things in their life as well—it shows that these people can juggle an awful lot."

So, How Does the Interview Process Work?

"We send school teams (have name tag, will travel) out to the colleges. For the first cut, what's most important is their ability to maintain poise, and to recognize what the situation is all about—the ability to step out of the situation, and say, 'What do we both want to get out of this?' This is an ability that a lot of these kids have already acquired because they've worked in financial institutions during the summer, and they've done a lot of homework—not so much, 'let me tell you what your stock price is'—I mean, that's nice, but it's even more important if they've figured out how they're supposed to conduct themselves, found out what people in my field think is important.

"We choose who we're going to call back and then they go through a second interview, and then a third interview. They're going to meet a bunch of different people at these interviews, and in some ways we're all very much the same, but in other ways we're very different. We sit down later to compare notes and discover if candidates rehearsed. To some extent a lot of interviewers are going to ask the same questions over and over again. Students

---

A point of view

"I'll ask them if they watch the show, and if they do I'll ask, 'what would you change to make it better?' I'm looking for a point of view. I don't want them just to say, 'It's great. There's nothing to change.' And I hope they're smart enough not to lie, because I'll know immediately."

(Television producer)

should try not to sound tired or bored. We're just as tired as they are.

"They don't see me until their third interview."

Do You Turn up the Pressure on Purpose?

"Good interviewers don't do that. Usually, the stress is already there. A good interviewer recognizes that she is selling her company. Even if the guy you're interviewing is the worst person in the world, his best friend may be the best candidate in the world."

How Do Students Sabotage Themselves?

"People tend to slip into generalities. Be prepared to back up everything you say. I catch people all the time. They'll say 'Oh, I was really bored.' You were bored by what? *For example, I'll ask someone to tell me about his summer job, and he'll say, 'It was great.' You're thinking, does this person have a limited vocabulary, or is he just shy? Tell me why* it's *great. He'll say, 'Well it was just a great job,' and you're beginning to think he must be a complete airhead.*

"Approach these like essay questions—prepare. A lot of the career counselors at the schools do a good job of coaching, including videotaped rehearsals."

How Else Do Students Sabotage Themselves?

"The worst thing they can do is start badmouthing other employers. They have to be careful of the question, 'What was your most frustrating work experience?' I mean, I ask that because I want to find out if people are listening or conducting themselves appropriately. 'I learned something from it' or 'I discovered that was not the right environment for me and here are the reasons why'—these are more appropriate responses to that question."

What Was Your Most Frustrating Work Experience?

"Every once in a while you get someone who was a great interview but doesn't work out, and then you feel really bad about some of the great people you had to turn down."

Is Physical Appearance Important?

"Good eye contact is critical. Appearance is also very important. A Brooks Brothers pinpoint cotton shirt. That's what men wear here. A conservative suit for women. If you aren't comfortable wearing that to the interview, you probably won't be comfortable working here. Discipline and attention to detail are very important. Make your appearance a nonissue."

What Makes You Mad?

"Job hopping. I just got a resume today. The guy had switched jobs three times in the three years since college. I threw it in the garbage. I don't have time to read a resume that comes to me with no introduction and shows a lack of stability and commitment. I've heard applicants complain about other jobs: 'They didn't give me the level of responsibility I deserved.' Well, hey, you've got to earn it."

Do You Expect a Thank-You Letter After Every Interview?

"Unless they really connected with me, I think it's a little phony. I get so much mail. I don't have time to read two thousand thank-you letters. I mostly won't remember who did and who didn't send me one. This one I got today, though, was so good, I actually attached it to his file. It was very appropriate and sincere and helped to explain this candidate."

What Do You Consider Your Greatest Weakness as an Interviewer?

"I'm too compassionate."

Thank You. You've Got the Job.

And yet more resume blunders

Just another prude:

"Exposure to German for two years, but many words are not appropriate for business."

Yeah, but does he fetch coffee?

"Typing speed: 756 wpm."

(Source: Accountemps, 1992)

Surviving While You're Looking

Maybe you're starting early a little late, and you've decided to take an unpaid internship in the field you really want to break into. Maybe you've already done some internships while you were in college, but you haven't yet landed the job you want. Maybe you're going into a career in the arts. Maybe your parents have changed the locks.

In any of these cases, you are going to need what is called a "day job," at least for a while. This is a confusing term since many day jobs are actually performed at night. A day job is any kind of part-time work that enables you to eat and sleep with a roof over your head while you go about the serious business of your career.

What kind of standard of living should you aspire to during this phase of your life?

SQUALOR

It is going to be difficult. Many day jobs pay much too well. Well-meaning bosses will give you raises. Your own innate ability to do a good job is just going to

Macaroni and Cheese

(version #1)

    3/4 cup macaroni

    2 quarts boiling water

    3 tablespoons butter

    3 tablespoons flour

    1 cup milk

    1/4 teaspoon salt

    3/4 cup grated cheddar cheese

Add macaroni to water. Melt butter, add flour mixed with seasonings, and stir until well blended. Pour milk in gradually, while stirring constantly. Bring to boiling point. Boil 2 minutes. Add cheese gradually until melted.

(Source: *The Boston Cooking School Cook Book* by Fanny Merit Farmer, 1930 edition, Little, Brown and Company, Boston)

encourage them. However, through all this, you must firmly keep your head and resist every attempt people make to pay you a decent living wage. What you want is squalor.

You probably think we're kidding, but we're actually dead serious this time. Here's the problem: it is so easy to get comfortable just performing your day job. Day jobs are easy. You show up and do the work, and they pay you what seems like quite a lot of money. It's the immediacy that is so seductive. The immediacy of the money they pay you, the immediacy of the instant feedback—no waiting for the phone to ring or for someone to write back in response to a letter you mailed three weeks ago. The immediacy of a small complete world that will beckon seductively.

Compare that to your chosen field, in which, at the moment, nothing seems immediate. You have no paying job yet. People won't return your phone calls. You will have to fight for the opportunity to be rejected. In situations like this, your dreams can become disturbingly ephemeral, and you'll begin to wonder just what it was that you saw in whatever it was that you thought you wanted to do.

WHAT'S WRONG WITH BEING A PROFESSIONAL BABYSITTER?

Here is the most crucial, most critical thing we will tell you in this chapter. Nothing else we are going to say will be as important or as difficult to remember: no matter how much you don't feel like it, always make your real career more important than your survival career.

This will be hard because you won't always be getting very much agreement from the powers that be in your real career. In fact, you may not be getting any agreement at all. Your internship, at least in the beginning, may turn out to be nothing more than fetching coffee. Your job search may be yielding nothing but dead ends. Your artistic career may be resulting in nothing but rejection. And no one is going to be on your case about finding a way out from behind the coffee machine, or expanding your network of contacts, or joining an artist's support group in quite the same way that your restaurant manager or head carpenter or chief fact checker is going to be on your case to please work twenty-four straight hours just this once, because someone else called in sick, and "I'll make it worth your while."

This will also be hard because you can have an extremely exotic life working part time. Here is just a partial list of jobs some of the people interviewed for this book have taken to support themselves in lean times:

> fisherman, baby-sitter, bartender, waitress, office temp, proofreader, carpenter, phone operator, bouncer, telemarketer, process server, bicycle messenger, door-to-door salesman, fact checker, go-go dancer (be very, very careful), sperm donor, bird breeder, model mugger (playing the role of attacker for a women's self-defense class—$30 an hour), providing eggs for in vitro fertilization, writing pornographic novels, marrying an illegal alien to help her get her green card, gathering herbs in a forest for PepsiCo, teaching English to Russian immigrants, running errands for a cult, being a roustabout (which has the distinction of being among the top ten worst jobs in America, according to *The Jobs Rated Almanac*), crewing on sailing yachts that are being shipped from New England to the Bahamas for the winter season, handing out leaflets on the street

Doug McMullen has published a couple of short stories since he finished college. However, since most of the prestigious literary magazines pay only about $250 a story, Doug has been forced to support himself in other ways. Here are some of the things he has done to pay the rent: photographed people dressed up in Edwardian costume on top of the Empire state building; cut wildflowers in fields in upstate New York, drove back to the city and sold them to florists; worked for a photographer hand-tinting fleshtones on cherubs for fake 19th-century lithographs; operated spotlights for a circus; was a bike messenger; acted as chauffeur for a Japanese Kyogen group (like Kabuki); worked as a puppeteer and a bouncer—all of this in a two-year period.

HMM. WHAT WAS IT I SAID I WANTED TO DO?

We aren't saying that you shouldn't have fun during this time in your life. Lots of part-time jobs can be completely exhilarating and great seasoning for whatever you're going to do in real life. In fact, they can't help but broaden your horizons.

We're just saying that you shouldn't get comfortable. Don't let time go by unnoticed. Be rigorous with yourself. An internship is what you make of it. Finding a job is a job in itself. Forging an artistic career is one of the most difficult things you could ever hope to accomplish. It would not be unreasonable to expect yourself to devote several hours a day to your quest, at a bare minimum.

FORM A SUPPORT GROUP

It is almost impossible to do this all by yourself. You need a bunch of like-minded individuals surrounding you. It doesn't have to be a formal, organized group— just a bunch of friends who are going through similar trials and tribulations. If you are interning at a television station, there are probably several other interns working with you who are, after all, going through exactly the same experience you are. That gives you all a lot in common. Arrange to have get-togethers once a week so you can all bitch and moan and think up productive ways to get them to give you all more responsibility.

If you're looking for a full-time job, don't just hang around your employed friends. You need some other people who are going through what you're going through. If you're an actor, take classes with friends; go to auditions together. If you're a writer, take workshops; read your work aloud. Get feedback. And whatever you're doing, be sure to make the professional scene—meet the people in your profession, go to parties (particularly the ones with free food), join the professional organizations. All this will make you feel like you are a part of the life.

HOW MUCH MONEY DO I NEED?

Only as much as you need to get by on bread and water. If you find yourself buying toys to make yourself feel better, then you are earning too much money. No new car. No huge entertainment center. No taxis to work, or expensive vacations to take your mind off how bored you are to be working as a whatever.

If you luck into a hot restaurant or a good lobster-shift proofreading job, you can earn a lot of money. How much? It's difficult to get restaurant people to talk about it on the record, since so many of them are not declaring all their money to the IRS, but we hear some people are earning in excess of $200 a night.

"This is kind of embarrassing," **Lauren Battista** says of how she got her first job. "So many people in fashion did all the right things— went to FIT, studied the industry." Lauren had been a sociology major at Holy Cross College, and, "I really wasn't sure what I wanted to do. I had come to New York to interview for some advertising jobs, but then I heard about this fashion job through a friend of the family. I interviewed with the director of merchandising and the vice president all in one day. They called me two days later and offered me a position as an assistant merchandiser. I liked clothes and I thought it would be glamorous. Ha! Want to know my starting salary? $12,000. I shared a tiny apartment with two other people; I slept on the couch."

Just remind yourself, if you are making $200 a night in some trendy restaurant, you are already at the top of the restaurant profession. There is nowhere else to go from there. Well, if you're very unlucky, they'll make you a manager. And meantime, your real dreams are getting put on the back burner. Do this long enough, and they will just disappear.

If you do luck into a high-paying job, then make sure you do it only twice a week. Or save the extra money religiously so you can quit and pursue your real career full time.

SOCIAL LIFE

The idea is to keep things Spartan enough that you will keep the heat on yourself to accomplish your goals. On the other hand, if things get too Spartan, you'll be too depressed even to have goals. You'll need some entertainment. Fortunately, there's lots of free entertainment in every town. Most newspapers have a listing of free events each week. Then there are parties. When all your roommates (oh yes, you'll have roommates, which we'll discuss in the next chapter) invite all their friends, you will find that there will be almost a hundred complete strangers dancing in your living room. When it all gets too much for you, you can just hop a courier flight. Here's the way courier flights work: a company buys an airline ticket in order to use the baggage allotment to ship time-sensitive cargo quickly. In exchange for babysitting the claim ticket, you get to fly for much less than half the airfare. Every day the flights leave for all kinds of exotic locations, and the more flexible you can be, the lower the fare. The only real disadvantages are that you can bring only carry-on luggage, and if you are traveling with a friend, you will almost certainly be on different flights. However, this is probably just as well, because long flights can be very romantic, and that's the last thing you need.

WHATEVER YOU DO, DON'T FALL IN LOVE

There's nothing like a passionate, all-consuming love affair to ruin all the lovely squalor you've managed to build up in your life. For true squalor, you have to stay single and unattached, lean and mean. Maybe we're kidding a little.

WHAT KIND OF PART-TIME JOB IS BEST?

The major philosophical decision you'll have to make in choosing your part-time career is whether you want to do something related to your real field. There are some real advantages, if you can find a job you like. For one thing, you will be getting paid for something that is in at least the general ballpark of what you want to be doing. (For example, when actor Ethan Mintz graduated from college, he took a part-time job with an after-school program teaching drama to elementary school kids.)

For another, you may get either experience or the opportunity to meet someone who can help you in your career. Artist Ben Heijst took a job as an assistant to an established artist, and has met many important people through his job.

On the other hand, some people find that doing something related to their chosen career is too distracting. Fiction writer Lisa Kaufman decided that she was no longer interested in editing fiction for a major publishing house. She decided the editing was getting in the way of her own writing.

Here are some brief descriptions of some of the more popular types of part-time work.

OFFICE TEMPING

The pay is not much to write home about, but office temping can make up for what it lacks in money by the experience and the flexibility you get. The experience comes in two varieties. For those who haven't spent much time in an office, temping will give you a very fast lesson in the dynamics of office interaction, which can save you a lot of grief and misery when you finally land the job you're looking for. You'll also find that your word processing skills (which you're probably going to need even when you land the job you want) get much better with just a little practice.

The flexibility is built into the job. When you enroll

with a temporary employment agency (treat this like a real job interview and wear your best suit) you tell them when you are available for work. Within reason, they will find you assignments that fit your schedule. So, for example, you could set aside Thursdays and Fridays for interviews, and work the other three days a week to support yourself.

Once you get a reputation for being reliable, you will be allowed to be as flaky as you like. This might seem like a strange statement, but in the world of temps, if you show up for work on time and don't shoot up in the bathroom, you are already going to stand out head and shoulders above most of your colleagues. This often means that you will be offered full-time work by one of the companies you work for. While the salary increase may be tempting, you do not want to get sucked into a job you don't really want, especially if it makes it virtually impossible to continue your search for a job in your field. Full-time employees don't get Thursdays and Fridays off.

However, it also means that you are going to be well regarded at your employment agency, and this can be very useful. These are the people who decide who gets to interview for the plum full-time jobs. These are also the people who may be able to find you at least a temporary position at a company in your field.

As we said in chapter 9, going the temporary route may be particularly useful if you haven't decided what career to take up. By taking a series of short-term assignments in different industries, you can get a quick guided tour of the possibilities, while getting some valuable office experience and getting paid at the same time.

PROOFREADING

These jobs do not exist everywhere in the country, but there is a constant need for legal proofreaders in most large cities. Law firms produce reams of deadly dull memorandums, letters, and legal documents, all of which are supposed to be error-free. You'd think that the new computer programs out there would have made proofreaders superfluous, but they haven't. There is still a need for trained human eyes to read over this material.

Who has the shortest work week?	
	(hours per week)
Baseball Player	30
Waiter	36.2
Dishwasher	36.2
Cashier	37.2
Maid	37.9
Child care worker	37.9
Bartender	37.9
Receptionist	39.1

(source: The Jobs Rated Almanac)

The key word here is "trained." All of the want ads specify "experienced" proofreaders. Generally, the way to get past this is to either get recommended by a friend who is already working in the field is willing to teach you the proofing symbols, or to take a course in proofreading (these are often listed under the want ads masquerading as real jobs). Many of these courses promise placement services as well. You will find that the jobs they can find you are fairly low paid; however, the point is to get a bit of experience, and then quit and find one of the high-paying lobster shifts through the want ads, a contact, or an employment agency that specializes in proofreaders. These night shifts pay extremely well— we're talking $25 an hour or more, plus a taxi home at the end of your shift. Interviewing for these jobs is serious business. Dress the same way you would to a real job interview. Proofreading is a skill that you can take with you to another city if you move and that you can dust off if you are ever in need of money down the line. Perhaps the best part about proofreading jobs is that the best ones take place at night, which means your days are free to pursue your chosen calling. Sleep, of course, is optional.

RESTAURANTS

Working as a bartender or waiter offers the prospect of large amounts of money in a very short time. Restaurants also feed you fairly often, which helps to cuts down on your household expenses. The best way to find a restaurant job is to look for a crowded, fast-paced area of town with many restaurants, and then just start going door to door. The best times are in the morning between 11:30 and noon, and in the afternoon from 2:30 to 4:00. Ask to speak to the manager. She will want to know if you have any experience. Just say that you do. Restaurant managers are not so much interested in your experience as in your ability to lie brazenly. Later, this will come in handy when a customer asks if the fish is fresh or frozen. There is no one dress code when you are applying for a job. In certain restaurants, an earring worn through the nose is practically a requirement. Mostly, you should pick restaurants you feel comfortable dining in, and dress the way you normally would as a customer.

As with any job, you will have to pay dues by working the worst shifts at first. However, if you're good, you will find that you get to the lucrative shifts fairly quickly. Make sure that you don't let your choice of shifts be dictated by the amount of money they earn you, but by your career needs. If you are looking for a job in advertising, you won't have time to work day shifts at the restaurant. If you are a saxophone player, then you won't have time to work night shifts. The dangers of any part-time job are, if anything, amplified in restaurant work. It is much too easy to get comfortable and complacent working in a restaurant. You can make too much money, there is too much booze around, and there is an instant social world to surround you and tell you that it's all right that you haven't sent out a resume, or put paint to canvas, or gone on an audition in over a month.

TEACHING

Opportunities to teach keep expanding. There are adult education classes, English as a second language classes, SAT prep courses, martial arts courses, word processing classes. If none of these appeals to you, or if you don't feel qualified to teach any of them, think up a course of your own and sell it to your local adult education entrepreneur. Judging by the catalogs they put out, they seem happy to let just about anyone teach just about anything.

The pay can be quite high for some of these teaching positions, with the worst pay in general going to private schoolteachers, who often are not required to have lots of teaching credentials, and the highest pay going to public schoolteachers. However, unless teaching is what you want to do for a permanent living, you don't want to spend the time to take education courses at some local college in order to work full time at a public school, instead of pursuing your dream.

To find a part-time teaching job, look in the help-wanted ads. Most of these jobs entail more work than

John Canavan came to New York to become an actor. To pay his rent, John answered an advertisement in the Village Voice for a child care job. He found out that he was caring for the children of a cult. "The kids were very intelligent and very advanced for their age, but I think by the time they get to be in their teens they're going to need some serious therapy." John stuck it out for over a year until he "finally found some acting work."

Macaroni and Cheese

(version #2)

    1/2 pound macaroni

    8 to 10 tablespoons butter

    salt and freshly ground pepper

    1 to 1-1/2 cups shredded
    sharp cheddar cheese.

Cook the macaroni in boiling
salted water until it is just tender.
Be careful not to overcook it, lest
it become very mushy. Drain.
Butter a 2-quart baking dish, and
arrange in it alternating layers of
macaroni dotted with butter and
shredded cheese. Season with
salt and pepper, and top with a
layer of cheese. Bake at 350
degrees until the cheese is
melted and the macaroni is
heated through

(Source: *James Beard's American Cookery*. Little, Brown and Company. Boston 1972)

you might think at first. Generally, there will be some sort of training, and then there is the preparation for the class in addition to the actual time in the classroom. An advertised hourly rate usually only includes the hours that you are actually teaching.

Teaching can be enormously fulfilling, and also offers you the chance to practice your public speaking—a skill that will come in handy in practically any career.

ZEN AND THE ART OF MANUAL LABOR

There is something enormously satisfying about building something with your own hands. Some people find that no matter how cerebral their chosen occupation, if they have to do something on the side to support themselves, they would rather it be something physical. Working as a carpenter, or freelance plasterer or painter can pay quite well, and there is no need to dress up.

Most carpenters and painters find that they do better working for themselves, rather than for some large organization. By putting up notices on local bulletin boards, advertising in local newspapers, and getting the word out, it is possible to make quite a lot of money. Since most building has to be done during the daytime, this can put a crimp in your internship, interviewing, or daily artwork hours. It is a good idea to decide ahead of time to devote certain days of the week to your career, and stick to your schedule, no matter what.

A FINAL NOTE

If you have any sense of pride, you are going to get pretty good at whatever it is you are doing on the side— and this is not necessarily a bad thing if you keep it in perspective. The restaurants in Los Angeles are full of bad waiters who excuse their shoddy performance by saying, "I'm really an actor." Doing mediocre work can be habit-forming. If you get used to expecting less of yourself in the dining room, you may start expecting less of yourself in the job you really want. Doing the best that you can is never a waste of time.

Now let's talk about the nuts-and-bolts issues of living on your own.

The Practical Details of Living on Your Own

It doesn't matter whether you've found your dream job or whether you're just surviving while you're looking by working part-time—in the months after college, certain practical matters come up, some of them for the first time. We are talking taxes. Health insurance. Student-loan payments. Finding an apartment and signing a lease. Getting credit. Buying clothes for work. After years of protecting you from the harsh realities of life, your parents and society are suddenly going to expect you to know how to do all these things, apparently by osmosis. Here's a short primer.

TAXES

Whether you're working full-time at the job of your choice or part-time in a mall, you are probably going to be earning more money than you ever have before. In fact, when you first find out the details of your salary, you might think, "Wow, even *I* could live on this much money." Don't count on it. For one thing, you will be amazed to see how little of your salary ends up in your paycheck. You've had taxes taken out of your earnings before, but never like this. Unfortunately, the more you earn, the more that's taken away.

If there were no taxes or FICA in the United States, a single person earning $20,000 a year would receive a paycheck of $384.62 each week. As of this writing, what that person actually receives in "take-home pay" is $261.30 per week. Big difference.

There is one silver lining for anyone who starts working immediately after graduation: because of simplistic IRS formulas that withhold taxes based on the premise that your total earnings will be your weekly salary times fifty-two (even if you have just joined the labor force in June, and will only earn half a year's salary), the IRS will withhold far too much during that first half year, and you should get a fat refund next April.

However, don't get used to that refund, because next year, if you work the entire year, your withholdings should be about right, and you won't get much back from the government at all.

WORKING MORE THAN ONE JOB

If you're working several jobs, you should take care that enough money is being withheld from your paychecks. Many people who work two jobs get a rude awakening at the end of the year when they calculate their taxes and discover that they owe some huge amount of money they no longer have. Again, this happens because of simplistic IRS formulas. Each company you work for will withhold for you as if that is the only money you are going to earn all year. If you take on two part-time jobs, each of which pays you $10,000, your two employers will withhold a total amount of taxes that is much less than what would have been withheld if you had one $20,000 job.

To make sure you don't come up a couple thousand dollars short, you should change the number of exemptions you claim. An exemption is essentially a discount on your tax bill. Every unmarried person gets one exemption as a matter of course. Later, if you get married and have children or other dependents, you get more exemptions (and a higher discount). However, right now, anyone who has more than one job might want to change the number of exemptions on the W-4 form from "1" to "0." Your employer keeps your W-4 form on file. It is a simple matter to fill out a new one.

THE UNLIKELY AUDIT

Whatever your parents say, unless you are the heir to a fortune, or own property, you don't need an accountant yet. There are few if any tax loopholes that can be exploited by a new graduate earning less than $30,000.

Save all your receipts, however. Even if you don't itemize on your taxes (which means writing down all your expenses to help lower your tax bill), receipts can come in handy in the very unlikely event that you *are* ever audited.

We say "unlikely" because the IRS generally only goes after people who earn enough money to make it worth their while. Performing an audit costs the IRS several thousand dollars; this means that unless they think you owe more in back taxes than it would cost them to audit you, they are not going to bother. As a new college graduate, you don't have much to worry about.

COUNTING YOUR W-2S

At the end of the year, you'll get a statement from your employer called a W-2 form. This will list your total salary, how much was withheld in federal, state, and local taxes, and social security payments. When you file your taxes you have to include a copy of this form.

The only time this gets complicated is when you've worked for several different companies. Sometimes, when the amounts are relatively small, employers will forget to send you a W-2; it can also get lost in the mail. Keep track of how many employers you had in the past year, and how many W-2s you should be receiving. It may be tempting to avoid the hassle of tracking down an old employer by ignoring the money you earned from him. However, this can cause all kinds of bureaucratic snafus. If the employer was withholding for you, it is unlikely that you will owe any extra tax, but it is never any fun to open your mailbox and see a letter from the Internal Revenue Service.

Average starting salaries for college graduates	
Accountant at a small firm	$24,750
Advertising Copywriter	$30,000
Secondary Teacher	$26,077
Electrical Engineer	$33,000
Financial Planner	$27,000
Government Economist	$21,486
Private G.P. Doctor	$86,300
Software Engineer	$33,702
CD-ROM Producer	$35,000

(Source: Fortune Magazine, 1995)

ARE YOU AN INDEPENDENT CONTRACTOR?

If you're doing part-time work, some employers will try to maintain that you are what is called an "independent contractor." When you get your first paycheck, you'll think this is a terrific idea: there is no withholding at all. The employer simply cuts you a check for the full amount. Unfortunately, this does not mean you won't owe any taxes on the money you earned. It just means you'll have to come up with those taxes in April when you've long since spent all the money you earned.

Employers like this arrangement because it's cheaper for them. If you were a regular employee, they would have to pay part of your social security tax, and possibly, health insurance premiums as well. However, if you are an independent contractor, they owe you nothing beyond your salary. When you work as an independent contractor you should receive a form called a 1099 from your employer at the end of the year. Resist the impulse to crumple it up and throw it away. Your employer also sent a copy of this form to the feds. If you don't declare that money, bells will go off in Washington. These days, this is all cross-checked automatically by computer.

It is especially important to track down missing 1099s. Don't just assume an employer has forgotten about you. It is in her interest to deduct the cost of employing you, so she has probably filed the 1099 with the government. If no copy reaches you, that doesn't mean you aren't liable for the taxes.

The IRS has started to crack down on employers who maintain that their workers are independent contractors when they really aren't, so this practice may become less widespread in the future. We aren't saying you should turn down work unless your employer agrees to withhold taxes for you. But if you take that work, be sure to remember that you are going to owe some money at the end of the year. And if you are an independent contractor then you are going to be especially concerned about medical insurance.

HEALTH INSURANCE

We believe it was the famous Doctor Louis Pasteur who made an important medical discovery: the only people

---

College grads with no health insurance

1987–89

MEN 15.9%
WOMEN 16.3%

1990–91

MEN 29.5%
WOMEN 12.2%

(Source: Monthly Labor Review, 1993)

---

who ever get sick are the ones who let their heath insurance lapse. The rabies vaccine thing was just a minor revelation compared to this. You have to have health insurance. Don't even think about not having it. Don't even think about thinking about not having it.

We know, you're healthy as a horse, and you always look both ways when you cross the street. However, one uninsured illness can wipe out your entire family's life savings. If you've found a full-time job, then you will be picked up by your company's health plan. However, if you haven't found a job yet, or if you are working only part-time, you will have to make your own arrangements.

If You Haven't Found Full-time Work

Probably the best option is to continue your coverage under your parents' health plan. Most insurers allow parents to continue coverage for their children until the age of 23. Even though you are probably in a hurry to establish your independence from your parents, this is by far the cheapest alternative. If you are earning enough, you can start making the payments yourself.

A few insurers will take you on as an individual policy holder when you reach the cutoff age. Others will not, in which case you'll have to go shopping. There are a variety of options available. Blue Cross is a nonprofit insurer that is required to take anyone who applies. There is a Blue Cross organization in every part of the country. At the moment, you can sometimes get cheaper insurance through a private for-profit company. This is because these private companies are involved in what is called "cherry picking"—offering lower rates to young healthy people like you, while they refuse coverage to older high-risk applicants. Some states are threatening to legislate against "cherry picking" soon.

Choosing a Deductible

Health insurance costs more the lower the deductible you choose. For example, if you have a $500 deductible, any visit to the doctor or hospital that costs less than $500 will not be covered by the policy, and you'll have to pay it yourself. Similarly, if you go into the hospital

---

Percentage of large firms that paid total costs of health care coverage:

49% IN 1989
30% IN 1993

(Source: Money Magazine, 1995)

---

for an expensive operation, the first $500 will not be covered. If you choose a $1,000 deductible . . . well, you get the idea. The higher the deductible, the lower the cost of the insurance. Since you are mainly trying to avoid bankrupting your family in the event of catastrophic illness, you can afford to take a high deductible.

WHEN YOU LEAVE YOUR JOB

It doesn't matter whether you quit, get fired, or get laid off, under the provisions of a law known as COBRA (Consolidated Omnibus Reconciliation Act), your employers must allow you to continue your coverage under their health plan for up to eighteen months after you leave. You will have to pay for the privilege, but the employers must offer the coverage to you at *their* cost. This is always much cheaper than getting an individual policy. The idea, of course, is to tide individuals over until they find their next job.

Unfortunately, there is virtually no such provision to help pay your student loans when you are out of work.

STUDENT LOANS

As soon as you graduate, the clock starts ticking. The government gives you a six-month grace period to find a job and catch your breath, and then the bills start arriving. It's impossible for us to predict exactly what your monthly payments will be, since everyone owes different amounts borrowed on different terms. Just to give you a ballpark figure, someone who owes $15,000, at an average rate of 8 percent would have monthly payments of about $182.

The only way to defer these loan payments is to stay in school. As long as you are a full-time student at a university, you can keep those bills at bay forever. If you get a job and then later decide to go on to graduate school, your loan payments will be deferred while you are in graduate school, and resume as soon as you get out.

THE AGONY OF DEFAULT

The default rate on government guaranteed student loans is almost 22 percent at the moment. This might give you the erroneous impression that a default is no big deal. You should realize that a large portion of that 22 percent comes not from college loans, but from loans made to students of trade schools with three initials and two faces. These trade schools are often scam operations designed to fleece the federal government by preying on immigrants and poor people. A new arrival to this country may not understand the importance of his credit rating, but you certainly should.

When people get into economic trouble, they tend to get very reticent, and often don't ask for help. Even though you may feel embarrassed, it is much better to call your lender and explain the situation than to miss a payment with no explanation. Many banks will draw up new repayment plans, or accept a missed payment as long as you inform them ahead of time. For some types of loans (the Perkins loan is one), you can apply through your college for an emergency grace period, based on financial hardship.

It can take years to build up a good credit rating once you have loused it up. Meanwhile, you may not be able to get credit cards, and getting additional loans for graduate school can be difficult if not impossible.

201 chief executive officers were asked how likely it would be for their company to have a female CEO:

	in 10 yrs	20 yrs
very likely	2%	18%
somewhat likely	14%	63%
not very likely	42%	15%
not likely at all	40%	2%
not sure	2%	2%

(Source: Fortune, 1992)

STUDENT LOAN CONSOLIDATION

One option, according to Kal Chany, of Campus Consultants, is to investigate loan consolidation. "Many banks are willing to consolidate all your student loans from different sources into one big loan, often with lower payments than you were making before." In some cases, these new loans can be designed so that during the first few years out of school, you make interest-only payments (which are much lower). In other cases, the loans are set up so that you make graduated payments. In the first couple years, the payments are very small; then, as you get older, the payments gradually increase. If your original lender will not consolidate your loans, you can go to another bank. The new bank will essentially buy the loan from your original lender.

SAVING AND INVESTING

An entry-level salary generally does not allow you to do any meaningful saving. However, if you do have the odd hundred dollars to invest here and there, it would probably be smarter to use the money to make extra payments on your student loans or credit card debt. Look at it this way—many investments are earning less than 5 percent right now. Your debt is costing you at least 8 percent (for government guaranteed loans) and possibly as much as 20 percent (for many commercial credit cards).

By reducing your debt by $100, you are actually getting more bang for your buck than if you invested the same $100 in treasury bonds.

PLASTIC OR CASH?

Many people would rather use credit cards to buy things than the cash they have in the bank. "I know I could pay off my $1,000 credit card balance," people say, "but then I'd be broke." While this kind of thinking may make people feel better, it is actually incredibly dumb. As any accountant in the world will tell you, if you have $1,000 cash in the bank but you owe $1,000 on your credit cards, then you *are* broke. It may make you feel better to see the money in your bank account, but that doesn't alter your situation. Meanwhile, you're probably paying as much as 20 percent interest on the credit card debt, which means that holding on to the illusion that you have money in the bank is costing you an extra $200 a year.

This is a lesson that new graduates probably have to learn for themselves. It is so tempting to charge the things you want. No one is going to tell you not to—certainly not the banks that are throwing these cards at you. Just try to go easy, because those same banks will have no compunction about destroying your credit rating and repossessing your stereo if you get in over your head.

APPLYING FOR CREDIT CARDS

There are two *good* reasons to have credit cards: to cope with emergencies and to establish a credit history. You

The Fine Print	
Rate Summary	**Purchases**
Number of days this billing period	Before 12/14/94
	30
Balance Subject to Finance Charge	376.39
Period Rate	1.65000%
Nominal Annual Percentage Rate	19.80%
Annual Percentage Rate	
19.80%	

need a good credit history because someday you are going to want to borrow some mind-boggling amount of money to buy a house or an apartment or a car.

Of course, you probably already have a credit card or two. However, depending on what kind of cards they are, they may not help you to build a credit history. Many credit card companies issue cards to the college-age children of their customers with the understanding that the parents are ultimately liable for the bills. If your present cards are actually in your parents' names (and this may be the case even if your name is printed on the card), you are not building your own credit history, no matter how promptly you pay every month. Therefore, you need to apply for your own cards now.

Some credit card companies (American Express is one) issue cards to full-time college students while they are still in school. This is useful in that you won't have to prove that you earn enough money in order to qualify. As long as you make your payments promptly, you can keep that card forever, and they will never ask how much money you now make.

How Many Cards Do You Need?

It's hard to make a case for having any more than two charge cards. Many people get by perfectly well with only one. If you intend to pay your bills in full at the end of each month, then it doesn't matter what kind of interest rate the card charges. However, if you are ever going to carry a balance, you should find a card with a low interest rate. Some of the biggest banks offer the worst deals, often charging as much as 20 percent. However, it's possible to find VISA or MasterCard issuers who charge less than 10 percent on outstanding balances. Either way, you should find out about the grace period the bank offers you on new purchases made with the card. Some banks give you what amounts to an interest-free loan for thirty days if you pay your bill in full. However, if you only make a minimum payment, they compute the interest from the moment the purchase was made.

You may be thinking that we're being ridiculous talking about such small amounts, but these small amounts add up to some pretty hefty figures by the end of the year, and interest payments are no longer tax deductible. If you're like most new graduates, a few hundred dollars can make the difference between spending your vacation in the Bahamas or alone in your apartment renting movies.

Should you take advantage of the credit card offered by your local bank? It depends.

A LOCAL BANK ACCOUNT

If your job takes you to a new part of the country, it is perfectly possible to keep your bank account from home and do your banking long distance—that is, until something goes wrong. Trying to resolve a discrepancy in your monthly statement over the telephone is an exercise in futility you probably don't need to experience first-hand. The same goes for getting a store to accept an out-of-state check. It makes sense to open an account in your new location.

Since you're opening a new account anyway, you might want to choose the same bank your company uses. Not only will your payroll checks clear with alacrity but you also may have a small amount of pull when it comes time to apply for a car loan or a mortgage. Whether you take that bank's credit card depends on how good the deal is. The main thing you want is to get your local bank account set up as soon as possible. You are going to need it to write a large check to your new landlord.

LOOKING FOR AN APARTMENT

You may already have lived off campus while you were in school, but if you are looking for an apartment in a major city, be prepared for a few surprises. To paraphrase Winston Churchill, never has so much been paid for so little. While rents have fallen a bit in the past two years, space (as in, square feet) is still a valuable commodity in short supply. When the realtor takes you to see your first "charming studio," you will probably snort with derision. However, after a few months of city living, you will find that you have mysteriously changed. When you visit someone who proudly shows you the cubicle that passes for her bedroom, you will say, "Wow, a bedroom! And it has a window."

Whether you're living in an urban or a rural setting, you'll find that landlords tend to be much less casual than those you may have encountered in the neighborhoods near school. Most will run a credit check on you before they let you sign the lease. If your credit or job situation looks shaky, they may demand that you get "cosigners"—i.e., your parents—to guarantee the rent.

They will also expect you to write a check for first and last month's rent, and possibly a month's rent in addition as a security deposit. This may be the first four-figure check you have written. If you find the apartment through a real estate broker, there will be a fee as well, anywhere from 10 to 15 percent of one year's rent. All of this leads rather naturally to our next topic for discussion.

ROOMMATES

Many new graduates can't afford to live by themselves during their first year or so out of college. Before you stamp your foot and adamantly declare that you're tired of roommates and will do whatever it takes to live alone, consider the possible advantages. It's cheaper. It's safer (especially if you're a woman). It's good to have someone to talk to sometimes.

All right, we know you've heard your share of roomie horror stories. Maybe you have a few of your own. But that doesn't mean you won't find the perfect apartment mate: someone entirely trustworthy, filthy rich, who hates to talk on the telephone and who will introduce you to many fascinating members of the opposite sex and then move in with her boyfriend/his girlfriend, but keep on paying rent at your place, "just in case."

It is generally best to have both roommates' names on the lease. That way if one leaves the other can keep the apartment going. If your apartment is located in a marginal part of town, consider buying apartment insurance. It is extremely cheap—about $100 a year, and it covers the replacement of your valuables in the event of fire or theft.

CLOTHES

You may have a general idea of what you will be wearing to work, but you should never rush out and buy yourself an expensive wardrobe until you get a feeling for the unspoken dress code at your particular office. Slavish emulation would be cowardly, but a complete disregard for the rules of your new company is hostile. Men don't need ten suits; three will do the job, at least initially. If you buy medium-weight suits, you will be able to wear them during three seasons. Women have more *apparent* flexibility, but you should be attuned to the nuances of your particular workplace. For example, it may seem during your first couple days that lots of women at your office wear dresses instead of suits; however, you may discover as you get to know who everyone is that it is only the secretaries who wear dresses.

If you start work during the summer months, you may get a false impression of the level of informality in your office. Don't buy all your fall clothes until you see what other people are wearing.

Finally, let us be the first to introduce you to an important concept in business clothing: the sale.

A Career in the Arts

If the average American holds ten jobs in a lifetime, the average musician, actor, writer, or artist holds over a thousand. Every week a musician may do four or five separate jobs, each for a different employer. A fiction writer or artist, whether she is working on assignment or on her own, sells her wares one at a time. An actor wins one part at a time. And talk about job interviews; an actor who is really hustling hits ten to fifteen auditions *every week*.

You have to truly love what you do to put up with the uncertainty and constant rejection that are endemic to any career in the arts. There is no way to spare yourself: talent does not exempt you from the rejection. Preparation does not exempt you from the rejection. Even keen business savvy does not exempt you from the rejection.

You may say, "Oh yeah? What about Whitney Houston?"

Our mental picture of people in the arts generally comes from the handful that we see on television—the .5 percent who are lucky enough to get wealthy from their art. But the overwhelming majority of people in the arts never get wealthy; many barely make a living. The odds that you will be the kind of artist who has

In 1993, 28% of the 39,000 members of Actor's Equity earned less than $2,500.

In 1993, only 8% earned above $100,000.

(Source: Actor's Equity)

JOHN HILLNER

a huge beautiful loft in Manhattan, an agent who weeps with admiration when you give him your next masterpiece to carry over to the Castelli gallery (where it will immediately be sold for $200,000), and a place in the permanent exhibition at the Museum of Modern Art, are alarmingly small. The odds that you will be the kind of actor who turns up on *The Tonight Show* to talk about how the TV series and the movies are just so he can afford to do live theater off-off-Broadway are completely remote. The odds that you will be the kind of writer whose books trigger bidding wars by the various publishing companies, or the kind of musician who travels to her next gig by jet are practically nil. We are not trying to dissuade anyone from a career in the arts. But we want you to know what you're facing.

We decided that the best way to give you the flavor of life in the arts was to interview four people who have chosen careers in the arts: a musician, an actor, a poet, and an artist. The four are at different places in their careers. One of them happens to make a lot of money. Another is doing quite nicely. The other two don't yet support themselves by their art. But as you'll see, that really isn't the point. All four have achieved recognition in fields in which just surviving is a kind of victory.

In professions whose goal is often to make what you do look easy, a beginner might think that there is no work behind the performance. As you'll see in the interviews that follow, the amount of backbreaking work that was involved in each of these people's careers probably exceeds the work required to become a doctor or an analyst on Wall Street.

John Hillner's first brush with professional theater came when he was still in college at Denison University. He'd wangled a work-study assignment in New York as a gofer for Broadway producer Manny Azenberg. "I got to go along for out-of-town tryouts of a play called *Miss Moffit* starring Bette Davis. The show started out with hope and promise and ended up dying within seventeen performances. You watched it vaporize before your very eyes. It was a matter of having all your illusions shattered. There was no glamour, there was no nothing; it was just reality."

It didn't matter. He was hooked. After he graduated from college (a double major in theater and business—honors in both), he apprenticed at the Westport Playhouse in Connecticut, building sets and getting bit parts here and there. "My dad was saying, 'What's the deal here? You just got all this education and you're working for nothing?' We were getting paid sixty bucks a week." At the Westport Playhouse he met Tammy Grimes, the stage actress, and got to run lines with her once or twice. Apparently she was pretty impressed because two weeks later he got a call from Chicago. The actor who was playing her son in *In Praise of Love* was leaving the show. Did he want to do it?

> *"I had to be on stage in twenty-four hours. The job was for two weeks in my hometown, Chicago. I got great reviews. I got my equity card. I got my first professional checks." He waits a beat. "The checks bounced." Although the checks eventually cleared, it was a fairly prophetic beginning.*

> *"When I came back to New York I thought I'd be hired in a minute," he says, grinning ruefully. In fact, it would be five years.*

> *"I handed out leaflets, I built bookshelves, I sang a cappella on the street. Finally I got a job as a waiter. I had no experience, I just went in and lied. I didn't know a Mimosa from a Screwdriver but I walked out of there after my first night with maybe forty-nine bucks in my pocket and I thought, 'Heh, this is all right.' I worked there a long time, meantime taking classes and going on auditions. There'd be thousands of people on those open calls. I used to go with friends. We'd go down there at four o'clock in the morning to be the first ones there and start the sign-up sheet—in those days, there was a sign-up sheet—then we'd go home, get some sleep, come back at ten for the audition."*

"I had had enough positive experience from college to have the confidence to stick with it. Of course, you always have doubts about whether you're ever going to get to do it. But I guess youthful optimism really carries you through a lot. My dad would call me and say, 'You got a job yet?'

"Being an actor means not being able to do what you want to do to support yourself for a long time. In my case it took five years. I went through a period when I was getting very close to getting cast but not quite ever getting the part. It was terribly frustrating because you're thinking, what is it that I'm not doing? You'd get down to the last five people, and you'd get cut, and then back at the restaurant you'd have to wait on those same casting people half an hour later.

"But you deal with it. If you don't want to do anything else, then you deal with it. I'd been sowing the seeds for years. I'd auditioned for this one director for years. He seemed to like me a lot, but he kept not casting me. I got down to the final callback for They're Playing Our Song *[a Broadway play starring Tony Roberts and Lucie Arnez]. It was down to three other guys and me, and I thought, here we go again. But then they gave it to me."*

From then on, things got a lot easier. John had done four Broadway shows in a row when he got cast as one of the stars of a television series called *We Got It Made*. It lasted for twenty-two episodes. And then this weird thing happened.

"I thought I had the world by the tail. I'd done four Broadway shows, the series. I thought: I'm on my way." Then the show got canceled just as the Hollywood scriptwriter's strike hit.

"It was a very humbling experience to arrive at a certain place and think you're

*comfortable and then get slapped in the face
again. I almost had to take another survival
job. In fact, I actually built a few decks for
people. I was thinking of building cabinets
again, getting my carpentry tools together
again. If you have a fragile temperament and a
fragile ego, you're going to get very badly hurt
in this profession."*

At present, John Hillner has just finished doing a
New York production of *Company*. He is also apparently
in every third commercial on television. You can't help
but have seen him—a midwestern, wholesome face,
generally playing a young father, or a lawyer—about
as far away as you could imagine from the off-the-wall
character he played in *Crazy for You*—a performance
that has been described as a cross between Daffy Duck
and John Cleese. What is his advice for aspiring actors?

*"You need to keep auditioning to keep sharp.
The business is constant rejection. Every day, I
face rejection. You have to treat each audition
as an investment in your future. When I don't
get something I really wanted, I take my
twenty-four hours when I brood and I sulk and
all that, but I don't allow it to go any further
than that. Always take your lessons, read
plays. I just finished watching the entire series
of* I Claudius. *You examine the choices the
actors make. You see an actor make a
movement, a gesture, and you say, 'Ah, that's
a great idea. I would never have thought of
that.' Or you see him do something else, and
you say, 'That sucked. What a stupid choice.'
"You have to constantly watch good actors—
go see something off-Broadway, off-off-
Broadway, and you need to constantly
challenge yourself to get off your butt.
Audition every day. In a typical week, I do
about ten. There was one day last spring when
I had ten auditions in one day, and then I came
in to do the show. It was great. Generally, the
rule is you have to do thirty auditions to get
one job."*

You don't have to have a certain look to make it in this business. The character actors are the ones who work the most, who make the most money, and have no illusions about being a star. Being a working actor is what it's all about.

"You also need somebody to confide in, be it a spouse or a very good friend. You need someone to whom you can say 'God, I did a great audition today, but I know I'll never get it.' An actor with a family is a much more well-rounded person. My daughter Amy is my best critic. I used to take her to auditions all the time when my wife [actress Nancy Hillner] was out on the road. I'd ask her, 'What did you think of that? Was I funny?' And she'd say, 'Well Daddy, I think your first take was much better than your second take.' And you know, she was right."

The National Writer's Union accepts members in three levels: first level earning under $5,000; second level earning from $5,000 to $25,000; third level earning from $25,000 on up. Of the 3,300 members, "the vast majority" are in the first level, according to Marty Waldman, of the NWU.

It is clear as you talk to **Frazier Russell** that for him, poetry is not a career but a way of life. He spends his days working as the director of programs at *Poets & Writers Inc.*, a literary service organization. He teaches writing part time for the Writers Studio, and he is constantly going to readings and giving readings. A poet has virtually no chance of making a living from poetry.

"But for me, it's not just a matter of supporting myself. I like going to a job. Especially this job, surrounded by other writers. The prospect of going to a writer's colony and having nothing to do for a month but write is horrifying to me. I have a lot of friends who feel it's important to have jobs they don't have to care about. But for me, it's important to have a lot of passion about what my job is—and whatever power there is in the writing carries from what I do at this desk. I'm fortunate in that at this point I've integrated the pieces of my life.

"Many people say, 'If I had to work only part-time I could write more.' But most of the people I know, when that situation actually occurs, write less. I find that the busier your life is, the richer your life is, and it doesn't get in the way of the writing. The more things you imbue with your passion the richer the writing will be. You can always find time to write. You make time for it, you sleep a little less, you get it done."

Frazier describes his early development as a series of visits to bookstores: "Where I lived in Washington, D.C., there were great bookstores. And, I remember this very clearly, one day I discovered this Grove Press shelf. It had everything Grove Press had done. There was Samuel Beckett and Jean Genet and William Burroughs and those people. It was a whole new world." He went to New York University as a film major, but "I had a minor in ancient Greek, and I took lots of literature courses."

"There was a Brentano's that used to be on Eighth Street. I saw this book, Writings for an Unfinished Accompaniment *by W.S. Merwin. I didn't even know who W.S. Merwin was, but it was a nice-looking book, and I picked it up and looked at it, and I thought that someone had just given me this key. It hit a note, and I remember the next morning stuff was pouring out of me. Later, I found Paul Bowles'* The Sheltering Sky. *That altered me also, and I went on to study with Bowles in Morocco.*

"Like anybody who's just out of school, I sent out four poems to The New Yorker. *I had a friend who worked there at the time, so I asked him to put them in the in-box of the then– poetry editor Howard Moss. I figured, skip channels, let's go right to the heart. They were . . . uh, not great poems, but of course, I thought they were great. He was very gracious about rejecting them. And that was the end of my sending out for many years. I was just*

Poem by Frazier Russell

Their Names

Like boys from a creek
the dead come back

when you least expect it
like a man with a flashlight

in a cotton field at five a.m.
I too have spoken their names

like snow blowing the dead
who wear their deaths lightly

like a nightgown
summers of love and rum

and dusk like a dulcimer
set down in the grass

writing on my own, and reading a lot. I wrote
for some years in my twenties, and then I
stopped reading and I stopped writing for
three years. At that time, it seemed pointless."

Frazier was working for Ariel Books, a children's book packager. "I was working my way up the ladder, and ultimately ended up editing a number of lines of books for them. It was a small company so I got to do everything. I did that for six or seven years.

"Then I came to Poets & Writers, *four or five*
years ago. Suddenly I was surrounded by
seventeen writers and I got reminded fast that
writing counts, that this is an important thing.

"If you make the work as right as it can be, the
rest will follow. Over the years, I've met a lot
of writers, and my work is starting to get
known in some circles. Over the past couple of
years I've also done a lot of readings. The
more you do readings, the more people see
you, and the more they ask you to do more
readings. Then people know your work, and
ask you to submit your work.

"But it's all part of the process of taking
yourself seriously as a writer and making sure
the work is as strong as it can be. The mistake
for a lot of people is the desire to get published
right away. Make the work great, and it will be
undeniable. That doesn't mean it won't get
rejected. It'll get rejected plenty, but
someone's going to recognize the seriousness
of the work.

"Your friend will call up and say, 'I just got
published in Ploughshares *this month,' and*
there's a natural instinct to think, Gee why
wasn't I published in Ploughshares *this month?*
And that's good because it gets you thinking
about that, and you do need to think about

that. But then there's the unhealthy part which is, 'I'm worthless.' It's a continual battle. But if you make the work as strong as you can make it, then someone's going to see it."

Where does he see all this taking him? "I'd like to be able to put together a good book, and have it get taken, and then do readings—and most important I'd like the work to progress and get deeper."

How important is it to surround yourself with a sense of community?

"It's huge. Without that, it would be really hard. Most of us need or want a community of people who are like-minded. I don't mean in terms of aesthetics at all, but people who believe that what they do is important. One of the things they do at the Writer's Studio is give you a sense that what you're doing here is vital. It matters to you, it matters to us, your fellow students, and it matters in the world."

How often does he write? "When I'm working on a long poem, I'll write just about every day in the early morning before I go to work. But I don't beat up on myself for not writing if it doesn't happen. I know from experience, it always comes back. Young writers, when the day comes that the words don't come, they're terrified.

Any advice for those young poets and writers? "One of the prerogatives of life is you've gotta make a lot of mistakes and you've gotta do all the wrong things. Good writing is going on everywhere. Do you have to be in New York or Chicago or L.A.? Not to do good work. To get grants? I don't think so. The benefit to being in New York is that on any given night, there's fifteen different readings you can go to.

"I hope they can find a way to make it work for them. This life has worked for me so far. I love it a great deal, and I feel very fortunate."

Kathy Sommer got her first big break on the day she graduated from Yale. "I got a call from a musical director who I worked with in summer stock—he asked if I wanted to go out on the road with *The Magic Show,*

> **Local 802, the New York musician's union, reports that the average income of its 12,500 members is under $15,000.**
>
> (Source: *The New York Times*, 1993)

playing keyboards and being his assistant. I thought that was exciting, because my friends and I were joking about how I was going to be on food stamps, trying to make a living as a musician.

When that gig ended, Kathy came to New York:

THE HELEN HAYES THEATRE

MARTIN MARKINSON   DONALD TICK

DASHA EPSTEIN
HARVE BROSTEN   JAY S. BULMASH
present

ALISON FRASER   BARRY WILLIAMS
in

ROMANCE ♥ ROMANCE
Two New Musicals

Book and Lyrics   Music
BARRY HARMAN   KEITH HERRMANN
also starring
DEBORAH GRAHAM   ROBERT HOSHOUR

Scenic Design   Lighting Design   Costume Design   Sound Design
STEVEN RUBIN   CRAIG MILLER   STEVEN JONES   PETER FITZGERALD

Musical Director   Vocal and Dance Arrangements   Orchestrations
KATHY SOMMER   KEITH HERRMANN and   MICHAEL STAROBIN
KATHY SOMMER

Casting   Assistant Director   Production Supervisor
LEONARD FINGER ASSOC.   EDWARD MARSHALL   JAMES PENTECOST

Produced in Association with GEORGE KRYNICKI and MARVIN A. KRAUSS

Choreography
PAMELA SOUSA

Direction
BARRY HARMAN

Originally Produced by the Actor's Outlet Theater
The producers wish to express their appreciation to the Theatre Development Fund for its support of this production.

Original Cast Album on MCA Records & Tapes.

"I started coaching and getting my name around. It's probably easier to make a living for a pianist than it is for most other players. There are thousands of actors in New York who can't afford to pay their rent but they will pay for vocal coaching and accompanists. Then if you're good enough, and have the desire, you can break out of that and go into musical directing.

"My second real break was Cats—*the contractor knew my dad [drummer Ted Sommer] and the contractor's wife had heard me play at a recital."* Kathy was originally hired as a rehearsal pianist, but *"the moment we opened I started subbing on all three chairs, and then took over the 'keyboard one' chair when somebody left. I held that chair for six years. I really lucked into a show that ran for so long . . . well, it's still running even though I'm not doing it anymore . . . which afforded me the chance to get serious about my songwriting.*

"The only way you make it in the arts is no matter how bleak it looks sometimes, and no matter how low your self-esteem gets sometimes, there has to be something else to sustain you—a sense of drive that leads you toward the goal. Partly it's learning to really enjoy what you're doing. But it's also an aggressive need to get better at it. For me, I'm a perfectionist. You're always working your butt off to do it better, to get it right. I think I

got fired once in my life from a job, and it was so devastating. You think that you'll never put yourself in that position again, but of course you do.

"I also like earning money. I like being successful and the strokes that come with it. It's a real high when people recommend you. It makes you feel that you are somehow on the right track.

"Part of it is knowing when you're ready for certain jobs. I had opportunities to conduct earlier on and I never took them because I thought, maybe not yet. There's a time when you feel your skills are ready."

How does she prepare for a gig? "If I'm going to sub for a show I will sit down for three weeks and really practice. For instance, when I went in to sub for the Jerome Robbins show, I was practicing maybe nine hours a day. It's a matter of immersing yourself in the music. You have to do that because of the complexity of keyboard books these days. Even when I don't want to do a job, the lesson is that there's always somebody there who is connected to somebody else who is doing something that you *do* want and your name gets around as somebody who does a good job. Even when you take a job just for the money, you have to make it important enough that you do a good job and you respect the music."

These days a still very young Kathy Sommer can count herself as one of a very small handful of women who are regularly asked to conduct on Broadway. She has conducted for, among other shows, *Beauty and the Beast, Romance Romance, Cats, and City of Angels*, and she recently finished recording a cast album for the hot Alan Menken. What about the business end of things?

"As an artist, business is always something you're trying to avoid. It's more fun to be creative. I've always felt that I am not great at embracing the business world, but at the same time, I'm a real fighter, and I refuse to be taken advantage of. The question is always

how firm are you going to stand on something and how much do you want the job? Trying to find that balance is probably the hardest part of the business. I don't think you can survive without being good at standing up for the amount of money that you deserve. Of course, when you're just beginning, you don't have any negotiating power.

Mike Freedman grew up in Florida and went to New College, an alternative college in Sarasota, Florida.

"I had a double major in art and math. After I graduated, I couldn't decide what to do, so I went to Japan for a year, and studied Sho do—Japanese calligraphy. When I got back, I realized I'd forgotten all the math theorems, so I decided to become an artist."

Consul, Pen & Ink on paper, by Michael Freedman, 1992. Courtesy of the artist.

Mike stayed on in Sarasota and began painting seriously. "I got a grant from my grandmother," he says with a smile, "and besides, the cost of living in Sarasota was very low." He also began teaching part-time.

"Then I got connected with a gallery in Sarasota [the prestigious Corbino Galleries] and started selling some paintings. When I was first getting shown, my art professors from college said, 'Oh, you have to be careful or they'll ruin you.' I don't feel there's any conflict. I'd like to make a living eventually and be a successful artist. I don't think it would 'ruin' me."

Mike won grants from the Florida State Arts Council, the New Orleans Contemporary Arts Center, the National Endowment for the Arts and Rockefeller Foundation for a concept show based on a series of paintings of a blues singer. "If you have a good concept and you have a place to show the work and you have a nonprofit organization to back it, it isn't too tough to get grants. If possible, you want an idea that laymen can grasp—something gripping.

"Moving to New York has been a good thing. Not for selling my paintings—just the reverse, really— but for getting to see all the great things that are happening here. When I first got here, I would see a show at a gallery and say, 'Oh, my surface textures need work.' I had only seen photographs of the paintings before. But then you have to think, is that a good thing? I'm not always sure."

How does he feel about the trade-off between the need to make a living and having enough time to paint?

"I've gone through different stages. The job I have now, developing educational materials, is great because it's flexible, but it's not that flexible. I used to paint every morning. Now, because I have a lot of deadlines, I take full weeks off and paint for a week at a time. This has been a good month, though: I sold two paintings."

His advice for artists?

"Persistence. But I feel silly about giving advice, since I don't make a living from my art." He thinks about it for a minute. *"On the other hand, I've been doing it for six years and I guess that's a kind of success in itself."*

NINETY-NINE PERCENT PERSPIRATION

If you still want a career in the arts after reading these interviews, then you're crazy—and you may be an artist as well. But only time and a lot of hard work are going to tell.

Putting It Off

Sometimes, the only intelligent thing to do is to do nothing. If you just barely finished college, gasping for breath like a marathoner at the end of a race, it may be too much to expect of yourself to jump into a full-blown career right away. Maybe you are completely burned out. Or maybe you still just aren't sure what you want to do. If you've read this book up to this point and can't imagine starting your career right away, then nothing may be just what you need to do.

In spite of what your parents or others may have told you, it would not be the fatal act of a deranged madman to postpone your career for a couple of months or even a couple of years, so long as you have a plan. Buying a one-way ticket to Thailand does not constitute a plan. It is important to have some idea of what you want to accomplish with this time, even if your objective is simply to have fun. It is also important to impose some kind of time limit. Without a little structure, your temporary time off can become a debilitating permanent condition.

There are really three options. You could give yourself up to a year for what Elizabeth Tener of Smith College calls "floundering time." Since you probably have student loans to begin paying back, you will need to earn some money, but this doesn't mean that you can't have fun. You could travel to Japan and teach English. Or work as a *gentil organisateur* at a Club Med resort. Or take any of the fascinating part-time jobs we discussed in chapter 10.

Some students worry about what they will say later, when employers ask about a yearlong hole in their resume. There's practically nothing you can do that can't be explained later—it's just a matter of putting a good spin on it. Talk about what you learned during that time and how it has made you more responsible. Employers like to know that you've gotten your wanderlust out of your system *before* you start working for them.

The second option is to do something constructive while you flounder: join the Peace Corps, or one of the hundreds of other programs devoted to social change inside the United States or around the world. These programs sometimes ask you to sign on for as long as two years, but by all accounts the work is rewarding and you will have done something wonderful for your community, yourself, *and* your resume. *This* kind of floundering is considered extremely impressive by employers.

The third option, of course, is graduate school, which may or may constitute floundering, depending on your motivation for going.

Let's talk about the three options in more detail.

TAKING TIME OFF TO DO NOTHING IN PARTICULAR

Sometimes a period of brief inactivity can help to put your life in perspective. Even when you aren't consciously thinking about what kind of career you want, or where you want to live, or who you want to be, your subconscious will continue to ponder these questions. This doesn't mean that you don't have to take any responsibility for your future. Even while you are doing nothing in particular, you can still keep scanning the newspapers for articles about the subjects that interest you most. You can read trade journals, you can practice your word processing, and most of all, you can talk to everyone you meet who is involved in the field or fields that you are vaguely not thinking about.

WORKING ABROAD

Sometimes the farther away you get, the clearer your perspective. Traveling abroad has become a popular way to spend some time unwinding right after college. To give your trip some structure, buy a round-trip ticket, and book the return flight. Many countries require this— they don't want American ex-students running around indefinitely. But even if the country you're visiting doesn't require this, it's a good idea, anyway. In an emergency, you can sell the ticket. If you decide to come home early, the reservation can be changed. Most importantly, however, your trip will have a beginning, a middle, and an end.

In some countries it is possible to make a career out of being an American. In Japan, for example, there are almost 100,000 Americans earning a very tidy sum teaching English. Northeastern American accents are the most prized. Australians need not apply. The Japanese learn English in school, but the emphasis is on reading and grammar. While the average Japanese can put most Americans' knowledge of English grammar to shame ("Please excuse me, but is that a transitive or intransitive verb?"), most Japanese are very uncomfortable with spoken English. Americans get hired by the Japanese language schools to teach their students, among other things, how to swear.

In most of the Far East countries and some South American countries, there is a market for English instruction and translation. Each country has its own rules (written and unwritten) about work visas, which you flout at your own risk. Take the time to find out the right way to work in the country you are visiting. The American embassy is surprisingly unhelpful about getting you out of jail if it turns out you were breaking the laws of your host country.

If you ever start thinking about what it would be like if you remained in your host country and never went home, just take a look around you. In each of these countries you will find walking zombies—American teachers or translators who stayed too long. They have strange, faraway expressions in their eyes and ethereal personalities. After a while they start to walk with a limp and eventually they all go mad. So remember to buy your return ticket.

If in some countries it is possible to earn a living by "being American," there are other countries in which being from the United States has absolutely no cachet at all. For example, in most of the European countries it is almost impossible to find legal work unless you come in through a program or are hired in the United States before you arrive. For details on how to arrange work before you leave try:

Work Your Way Around the World by Susan Griffith. Vacation Work, Oxford, England (Writer's Digest Books: 1989), or the

Directory of Overseas Summer Jobs, edited by David Woodworth, Vacation-Work Oxford, England (Writer's Digest Books: published annually), or

How to Get a Job in Europe: The Insider's Guide, Chicago, IL (Surrey Books: n.d.), or

Passport to Overseas Employment: 100,000 Job Opportunities Abroad, Arco Books (Simon & Schuster: 1990).

GRADUATE SCHOOL

As the logical outgrowth of a burning interest to know more about a particular subject, graduate school is a wonderful thing. As something to do because you don't know what else to do, or because you want to put off entering the real world, graduate school can range from a waste of time to a truly awful mistake.

Family members may tell you that you can use a law degree in almost any field, but if you really don't want to be a lawyer, you are in for three years of misery. Friends may tell you that a B.A. is no longer enough, but without the drive inspired by a burning interest, graduate school will just burn you out.

And then there is the money. Graduate school is just as expensive as college, with one important difference: there are very few scholarships and grants available in graduate school. Most financial aid comes in the form of student loans, which means that ultimately *you* are going to be paying for every single credit.

If you aren't sure what to do, think about internships

Percentage of CEOs with
graduate degrees:

50.2%

(Source: Business Week, 1992)

or office temping in a number of different fields. Graduate school will still be there if you discover your burning interest.

GOOD WORKS

You can take time off to think, and do something wonderful at the same time. There are so many volunteer programs that it would be impossible to cover them all. We're going to describe briefly two programs for you (the Peace Corps and Teach for America) just so you get a sense of what is available. For a complete list of all the different programs, you should consult any of the following books:

Directory of Volunteer Opportunities, edited by Ellen J. Shenk, Career Information Center, University of Waterloo, Ontario, 1986.

Invest Yourself: A Catalogue of Volunteer Opportunities, edited by Susan G. Angus, Commission on Voluntary Service and Action, New York, NY, 1984.

Volunteer! The Comprehensive Guide to Voluntary Service in the U.S. and Abroad 1990–1991 edition, edited by Adrienne Downey, Council on International Educational Exchange and Commission of Voluntary Service and Action, New York, NY, 1990.

Alternatives to the Peace Corps: Gaining Third World Experience, Institute for Food and Development Policy, San Francisco, CA, 1990.

"People ask me, 'If I take a year off, does that mean I'll never get a job?' Of course not. This is the only time in their lives when students can do this."

—Head of an Ivy League University
Career Placement Service

THE PEACE CORPS

Set up by John F. Kennedy, the Peace Corps sends 3,500 college graduates every year to ninety economically disadvantaged countries to help in the areas of education, health, agriculture, and the environment. Admission to the program is competitive. Last year there were 220,000 inquiries for the 3,500 postings.

When the Peace Corps started, it was enough to have a B.A. and a great attitude. These days, applicants are going to be a lot more likely to be accepted if they bring some further qualification along with them: a teaching certification, a master's in education, a background in languages, engineering, nursing, forestry, or the environment—any of these will make you more valuable and help your application. A spokesman added that it was not out of the question for a strong candidate with just a B.A. to be accepted. "We interview every applicant."

If you are accepted, you sign on for a period of about twenty-seven months—three months of training, and then two years in the field. Assignments can range from farming in Poland to setting up a health clinic in Kenya. You receive a monthly stipend to cover expenses, and at the end of your assignment you receive $200 for each month of your service—about $5,400. If you're worried about how you would make student loan payments during this time, relax. Government guaranteed student loans are deferred during the time you are on assignment. In fact, some types of student loans (notably the Perkins loan) may even be partially forgiven—wiped off the books— by serving in the Peace Corps.

Still, this is not for the fainthearted. Conditions can be very primitive. Just the list of shots and inoculations you have to take to go to some of these locations is enough to give even a brave soul pause. And there is no guarantee that, should you need to visit one, there will be a hospital near enough to be of any use or, even if it is nearby, that it will have any medical supplies.

Nevertheless, ex-corps members talk about it as one of the great shaping experiences of their lives. Call 1-800-424-8580 for information.

TEACH FOR AMERICA

Begun in 1989 as founder Wendy Kopp's senior thesis, Teach For America is designed to get America's brightest back into the classroom as teachers in educationally deprived areas. The program looks for new graduates with demonstrated leadership skills, who are not yet in education but who are willing to devote two years to teaching in one of twelve locations around the country. Again, admission to the program is competitive: in the past three years, 8,600 people applied for a total of 1,800 slots in places ranging from the urban sprawl of Los

Angeles to remote areas of Arkansas. The application process involves two essays and a full day of interviews, during which applicants must do some actual teaching. Once hired, teachers in the program are paid a standard teacher's salary based on the geographical area that they are in.

The founders of the program hope that some of these people will continue as teachers, but even if you don't you will have helped to alleviate what is acknowledged to be one of America's major areas of weakness, and challenged yourself along the way. Call 1-800-832-1230 for information.

You Got It. Now What?

The moment you have waited for: they want you. You have won. Unfortunately, the news will often come over the telephone, so a war whoop may be out of the question. Elation is fine, but jumping up and down while screaming "I got it! I got it!" can seriously undermine your negotiating position. An interesting double standard will now emerge. After dragging their heels and making you come in for three interviews while they tried to make up *their* minds, they are now going to be in a tremendous hurry for you to make up yours. In fact, they may try to pressure you into accepting right then and there over the telephone. Let them hear your measured elation—but don't give in to the pressure. Ask for a few days to think it over.

WHY NOT JUST SAY YES?

Now, it's true that if you have done your homework along the way, you have targeted only the companies you were really intrigued by anyway. Presumably, if it has gotten as far as an interview, you were already pretty interested in their job. So you may be saying, "Why shouldn't I accept right away?" There are several reasons.

One, as we said in chapter 10, the interview really is a two-way street, and during your various meetings with representatives of the company, you may have learned something that gives you pause. Maybe you totally hate their working environment. Maybe you can already tell your personality will be thwarted at every turn by their corporate philosophy.

Two, if you have any other irons in the fire, you may want to try prodding these companies into action with the news that you now have an offer. They wouldn't be human if they didn't suddenly want you more. Employers are just as insecure as anyone else. The fact that someone else is willing to hire you makes you infinitely more desirable to them. However, if one offer *does* lead to another, be careful not to string anyone along. As soon as you've definitely decided on one company, get in touch with the other and let them know your plans. You don't want to burn bridges or alienate a company you may want to work for at some other time.

Three, employers respect deliberation. It will do you no harm—in fact, it may do you some good—to ask for a few days to think over this very important decision.

WHAT ABOUT MONEY?

Up until this moment, you have had no leverage. As we said in our chapter on the interview, any discussion of money is better postponed until after they have decided they actually want you. This is the moment when you are (temporarily) in the driver's seat. They have expressed their willingness to acquire you, but you haven't yet agreed to be acquired. If there was ever a time to ask for an increase in salary, this is it.

However, you should try to be realistic. You are an entry-level hire, and entry-level salaries are traditionally low. By now you probably have an idea of what the range of starting salaries is in your field. If the offer you have received is at the high end of the industry standard in your area, then you are probably better off not haggling. If the offer is at the low end of the range, then you should consider several things before you start haggling.

**Finding out
starting salary ranges
in your profession**

1. Ask contacts in the field.
2. Study the help-wanted ads for comparison.
3. Read trade journals and newsletters.
4. Consult reference books:
   The Occupational Outlook Handbook
   The Jobs Rated Almanac
5. Ask at your college career center.

Large corporations can afford to pay more than small start-up companies. On the other hand, small companies tend to promote faster, and sometimes reward their best employees with other forms of compensation such as stock options or bonuses. Large or small, any company in the midst of a lean period will aggressively be trying to cut costs. If you think the market will bear a slight increase in your salary, be prepared with facts and figures to back that up. Point out that their offer is at the low end of the scale, and that your qualifications put you at the high end of the scale. However, it is never a good idea to be confrontational. Rather than present them with a take-it-or-leave-it proposition, keep the discussion lighthearted. "I was thinking more in the range of . . . ."

Your prospective boss has only so many thousands of dollars budgeted for your salary. If you ask for more, he will have to find that money from somewhere, and possibly he may have to go to *his* boss and ask for permission. You'll have to size up the situation. If he starts looking intensely uncomfortable or embarrassed, this may be a situation that he feels is outside his control. Or he may just be a very skillful negotiator.

A good reason to try to be at the top of the starting salary range if you are working for a big company, is that raises are often cut in stone. Thus if you start out lower than some of your peers, it is going to take years to catch up, regardless of your performance.

INSTEAD OF MONEY

If your employers don't seem willing to budge on the salary question, or you don't feel you can ask, there may be some valuable concessions you can get them to agree to instead. Most salary reviews come after the first six months on the job. Ask for a three-month salary review, in lieu of more money now. The unspoken message behind this request is that you are going to be so valuable to them so quickly that they will be willing to give you a raise after only three months. Employers like the sound of that—along with the implied promise that you intend to work your butt off to earn it.

The number of vacation days you get will almost certainly not be negotiable, but the timing of your vacation may be. If you have always wanted to go to New Orleans during Mardi Gras, or view the only full eclipse of the sun in your lifetime from a plane over the North Pole, then now is the time to bring it up. Generally, new hires are expected to take their vacations when it is convenient for the company, but if you pin the dates down now, you will probably get to keep them.

You may also be able to negotiate the starting date of your employment. Of course, *they* want you to start tomorrow. However, instead of (or as well as) a higher salary, you can often bargain for a few extra weeks before you begin working for them. Remember, you aren't going to be eligible for a vacation for a long time to come—in some companies, it will be a full year. So a couple of weeks right now may come in handy. You can charge up your batteries, put together a wardrobe, and brush up on all the things you said you knew how to do on your resume.

How Will I Know If This Is Right?

Who has the cushiest offices

1. Attorney
2. Senator/Congressman
3. Bank officer
4. Advertising account executive
5. Public relations specialist

(Source: *The Jobs Rated Almanac*)

Most people are elated by a job offer, but you may find that you are immediately filled with foreboding. Sometimes this is a warning sign from deep inside your gut telling you that this job is truly not for you. Sometimes this is merely a warning sign that, like Groucho Marx, you are the kind of person who would never belong to a club that would accept you as a member. You will have to decide if your doubts are reasonable. It helps to talk out the positives and the negatives with someone you trust.

If you're worried about making the right decision, let us put your mind at ease: no one could possibly be qualified to decide anything as important as this without being able to see into the future. Since no one has a crystal ball, momentous decisions are, in a way, the easiest ones to make. Flip a coin, and remember that you can always change your mind.

Making a Good First Impression

Your first weeks on the job are going to be exciting and frustrating. Exciting, because you're at the threshold of your career. Old people always say that youth is wasted on the young. Well, those old people have just forgotten how great being young felt when they were young. There is nothing more electric than walking through the doors to start your meaningful career-launching job for the first time.

Frustrating, because you don't really know anything yet, and you will keep having to ask annoying questions of busy people who all seem to know what *they* are doing. Don't be shy; ask as many questions as you want. How else are you going to learn? It helps to spread your questions around, so that you aren't bothering just one person.

Ask for frequent feedback from your boss. It is sometimes hard in the beginning to know if you are covering all the tasks you are supposed to be covering, and how well you are doing them. Some bosses are better than others at letting you know. So when in doubt, ask.

GETTING ALONG WITH CO-WORKERS

Your work is going to be infinitely better if you have the support and goodwill of your co-workers. Take the time to compliment people when they do something well. If a secretary writes a good letter, if a colleague does a great presentation, if your boss handles a situation adroitly, let them know that you noticed.

It is almost never a good idea to complain or badmouth or get into a palace coup at any time, but certainly it would be incredibly dumb to do so before you know who is who. Take the time to figure out what's going on. Who's good at her job, who doesn't care, who are the real comers in your department? If you want to be included in that last category, you will have to learn what these people do to make themselves successful.

If possible, find someone at the office whom you admire, and try to emulate that person. How does *she* handle your boss's impatience? When does *she* step in if an intern is screwing up? You don't have to admire her from afar. Ask her to lunch, and see if the two of you hit it off. If you become friends, she'll be able to give you terrific advice as you face the pitfalls and pratfalls of your first year on the job.

Sexual harassment in the workplace

According to a survey conducted by *Working Woman* in 1992, more than 60% of its readers reported that they had been sexually harassed.

(Source: *Working Woman*, June 1992)

OFFICE SEX

Friendships at work have a slightly different dynamic than outside friendships. On the one hand, you are going to have a lot in common with co-workers, and it is only natural that you will become friends with some of them. On the other hand, you need to preserve some degree of decorum. It's difficult to maintain professional respect when the entire office knows you danced naked on top of a Chevy the night before. We aren't saying that you can't dance naked whenever you want to, but you may want to do this with other friends. At work, you don't want to get *too* closely involved with anyone, particularly early on, and even more particularly, sexually. Working closely with someone on a tight deadline can be very exciting, but the negatives involved in an office romance are more numerous than you can possibly imagine before you actually get into one; do yourself a favor and keep all office relations platonic at least until you've become an expert at office politics. This takes four years. Don't ask why. It just takes four years. And you will need to be an expert to get through the next few months if you sleep with a co-worker.

Let's put it this way: sex at the office is fine just so long as it's not with an underling, a colleague, or a superior.

MAKING YOUR MARK

Once you figure out which individuals are great at their jobs, you can try to get yourself assigned to their projects. Obviously, these are people from whom you can learn. For the most part, seasoned employees enjoy being hero-worshiped, and will be glad to let you sit at their feet. They are going to take it less kindly if you start second-guessing them. Like everyone starting out, you are probably in a hurry to make your mark. However, you should stifle any desire to start rocking the boat until you thoroughly understand a situation.

Let's say you notice that by switching to another supplier, you could save the company $5,000 a month on raw materials. However, when you modestly bring this to your boss's attention, chances are you will find out that there are some very good reasons why they went with a more expensive bid. It could be that the cheaper company has been unreliable in the past. It could be that the supplier they use comes in cheaper overall even if that item is more expensive. Before you make a suggestion, you should do your homework to avoid looking stupid. And if you *are* going to propose a radical departure, it helps to have enlisted some support in advance, and even more important, it helps to be right.

CONSISTENCY

Every day, your performance at work helps build a network of people who think you are a consummate professional and fun to be around. Professionalism is often judged by consistency. It won't matter if you are brilliant every once in a while. People want to know who they're going to get when they walk into your office. Here are a few maxims: always be on time to appointments. Be sure to return people's phone calls, especially when you don't want to. Never lose your cool. Stay at work until the job is done. The fun-to-be-around part is judged not just on your sense of humor but on your consideration. When the pressure is on, who still remembers to say hello? Who still retains a sense of self?

FEET OF CLAY

We all know the feeling when we discover that someone we looked up to is actually only human. Inevitably, you will discover that your boss is not perfect. It is easy to go from adulation to contempt in ten seconds, but take a moment to talk to yourself. No one is going to be great at everything. Rather than think ill of him, figure out a way to help. Is there some nonthreatening action you could take that would make his life easier?

As you get to know anyone, you will spot weaknesses. Without being confrontational, you may be able to complement his performance with your own strengths. For example, if he is a great conceptual thinker but lacks organization, you can become his organizer. If he has trouble delegating authority, you may be able to change his thinking about you at least by asking to let you sink or swim on some small project—tell him you want to prove to *yourself* that you can handle it.

Every boss will have his problems. You can complain about it, or you can see it as a useful chance to take a look at yourself. What would your weaknesses be if you were in his situation? And how can you guard against letting these weaknesses cripple your performance when it's your turn to be the boss?

WALKING THE LINE BETWEEN SUPPORTING YOUR BOSS AND BEING A SYCOPHANT DOORMAT

Up to a point, if your boss looks good, you look good. Thus it is in your interest to support him in every way you can. His glory is your glory. On the other hand, if you do this too well, you will become indispensable and he'll never want to promote you. Always look for ways to shine. *Most* bosses will give you credit for your initiative.

By the same token, if all your boss wants is a yes-man or woman, start planning your transfer. Nothing good will come of your working for someone who refuses to hear bad news.

WHEN IT'S TIME TO START LOOKING AGAIN

When you are ready for your next job, your network—all the people who think you are a consummate professional and fun to be around—is going to spring into action for you.

And if they don't?
Well, there's always your parents' money.

Directories and other Job-Search Resources

To immerse yourself in a profession, it helps to read what the professionals read or have read. While we can't cover every field, the listings that follow should provide a starting point for exploration of some of the more popular professions. Remember, each field has its sub-specialities, and many of these have their own journals and trade newspapers. For a complete listing of periodicals, consult the *Gale's Directory of Publications and Broadcast Media,* available at many libraries. For a more comprehensive listing of internet sites, consult a directory such as Yahoo (http.//www.yahoo.com).

ADVERTISING

Advertising Age—twice-weekly magazine

The Standard Directory of Advertising Agencies: The Agency Red Book. National Register Publishing, Willmette, IL, published three times a year

Advertising Career Directory by Bradley J. Morgan. Visible Ink, Detroit, MI

How to Put Your Book Together and Get a Job in Advertising by Maxine Paetro. The Copy Workshop

Thirty Seconds by Michael Arlen. Farrar Straus, New York, NY (A great book describing the making of one commercial)

Confessions of an Advertising Man by David Ogilvy

THE ARTS

Backstage

FYI—quarterly newsletter published by New York foundation for the arts, listing grants and opportunities "for those who create and work in the arts." 155 Ave. of the Americas, New York, NY 10013-1507

Artsearch—monthly magazine with performing arts classifieds

Poets & Writers—monthly magazine

Money for Artists: A Guide to Grants and Awards for Individual Artists, Laura R. Green, editor. American Council for the Arts, New York, NY 1987

Artist's Market, edited by Susan Conner. Writer's Digest Books, published annually

Writer's Market, edited by Geneda Tennant Neff, Writer's Digest Books, published annually

Photographer's Market, edited by Sam Marshall. Writer's Digest Books, published annually

The Backstage Handbook for Performing Artists. Sherry Eaker, editor. Back Stage Books, New York, NY, 1989

BUSINESS

The Wall Street Journal, Business Week, Fortune, Forbes

ABA Banking Journal—monthly magazine

Marketing and Sales Career Directory by Bradley J. Morgan Visible Ink, Detroit, MI

The Insurance Almanac: Who What When and Where in Insurance. Donald E. Wolff, editor. The Underwriter Printing and Publishing Co, Englewood, NJ, published annually

The National Directory of Corporate Training Programs. Ray Bard and Susan K. Elliott, editors. Doubleday, NY, 1988

Standard & Poor's Register of Corporations, Directors and Executives. Standard & Poor's Corp., New York, NY, published annually (lists corporations naming principal executives)

Harvard Business School Career Guides. Harvard Business School Press, Boston, MA

Liar's Poker by Michael Lewis (a great book describing the inner workings of an investment bank at the height of the giddy eighties)

DESIGN

Progressive Architecture, Interiors, Interior Design

EDUCATION

The New York Times, Sunday Week in Review section

The Handbook of Private Schools: An Annual Descriptive Survey of Independent Education. Porter Sargent Publishers, Inc., Boston, MA, published annually

Directory of Public School Systems in the U.S. Association for School, College and University Staffing, Inc. Addison, IL, published annually

FASHION AND DESIGN

Women's Wear Daily, W (monthly version of *Women's Wear Daily*)

Vogue (including European versions), *Bazaar, Mirabella, Elle, GQ.*

Film and Television

Variety, Los Angeles Times, Backstage

Ross Reports (listing of who's who in television, current shows, agents) Television Index, Inc. 40-29 27th Street, Long Island City, NY 11101

Action—trade publication of Director's Guild of America 1516 Westwood Blvd., Ste. 102, Los Angeles, CA 90024

The Backstage TV/Film and Tape Directory, Back Stage Publications, New York, NY, published annually

Adventures in the Screen Trade by William Goldman. Warner Books, New York, NY, 1983 (a great book describing the inner workings of the film business)

GOVERNMENT

The Washington Post

Roll Call—a weekly newspaper devoted to government doings in Washington, D.C.; includes classifieds

The Federal Jobs Digest, P.O. Box 94 Millwood, NY 10546-9989, published bi-monthly

Working For America (Employment Opportunities in Federal Civil Service), Barron's Educational Series

Government Jobs and Careers by Ronald and Caryl Krannich. Impact Publications, Woodbridge, VA

MEDIA

The Columbia Journalism Review, Editor and Publisher, The New York Times, The Washington Post, The New Yorker, Spy Magazine, Vanity Fair

NewsMedia Yellow Book of Washington and New York: A Directory of Those Who Report, Write, Edit and Produce the News in the Nation's Government and Business Capitals. Monitor Publishing Co. New York, NY, published semiannually

Television & Cable Factbook. Television Digest Inc. Washington, D.C., published annually

All the President's Men by Woodward and Bernstein (great book detailing the Washington Post's coverage of Watergate)

MUSIC

Billboard magazine, BMI Magazine

Songwriter's Market 1993 edited by Mark Garvey. Writer's Digest Books

NONPROFIT

Community Jobs: The Employment Newspaper for the Non-Profit Sector. Write to Access: Networking in the Public Interest, 1601 Connecticut Ave., NW, Room 600F, Washington, D.C. 20009

Non-Profit's Job Finder by Daniel Lauber. Planning/Communications, River Forest, IL

Good Works (A Guide to Careers in Social Change) by Jessica Cowan. Barricade Books, NY

PUBLIC RELATIONS

Jack O'Dwyer's Newsletter

O'Dwyer's Directory of Public Relations Firms, J. R. O'Dwyer. New York, NY, published annually

Variety, Vanity Fair, the newspapers

PUBLISHING

Publisher's Weekly

The New York Review of Books

The New York Times Book Review

SCIENCE AND TECHNOLOGY

Each separate field has its own journals and periodicals, but here are some general works:
Scientific American, Cell

Peterson's Job Opportunities for Engineering, Science and Computer Graduates published annually, Peterson's

INTERNET SOURCES

The Online Job Search Companion (McGraw-Hill) by James C. Gonyea.

Be Your own Headhunter Online (Random House) by Pam Dixon.

On the World Wide Web:

http://www.infi.net/cwt/jobs.html

http://www.yahoo.com/yahoo/business/employment/jobs/

http://www.globaljobnet.com/

ABOUT THE AUTHOR

After attending Dartmouth and Columbia, GEOFF MARTZ worked as a musician and television composer for several years. He joined the Princeton Review as a part-time writer and teacher in 1986. Martz headed the team that designed the Princeton Review GMAT program, now taught in over fifty cities across the United States. He is the author or co-author of *Cracking the GMAT*, *Cracking the ACT*, *Paying for College*, and *Cracking the GED*.